EHANAMANI
"WALKS AMONG"

Ehanamani
"Walks Among"

An Autobiography
by Dr. A.C. Ross

BEAR
Kyle 1992

BEAR, Publisher
Box 346
Kyle, SD 57752

Printed in the United States of America

First Edition, 1992

Cover design by Walt Pourier
Original artwork by Martin Red Bear
Editing, design and layout by Jean Katus

Library of Congress Catalog Number 92-81334
ISBN 0-9621977-1-8

Dedicated to my best friend
DOROTHY BRAVE EAGLE
in appreciation of her selfless love
and enthusiastic support
through the years.

ACKNOWLEDGEMENTS

All Sun Dancers
All Tribal Medicine People
All Sweat Lodge Warriors
My Parents - Harvey and Agness Ross for their support
My Cover Artist - Walt Pourier
My Illustration Artist - Martin Red Bear
My Editor - Jean Katus
My Typist - Debbie Stuck
My Children: Dana
              Dawn
              Cindy
              Sandy
              Hok
              Fred
My Grandchildren: Krystal Dawn
                    Santee Kay
                    Kelsea Lynn
                    Katlyn
My Hunka Children: Amber No Horse
                    Ralphie Hernandez
                    Kristi Blue Bird
                    Chaskē Luger
                    Elgin Head
                    Stanley Natchez
                    Florentine Blue Thunder
                    Joe Marino

COVER DESIGN

Walt Pourier
Oglala Sioux Tribal Member
Illustrator
Image Systems
Boulder, CO

ILLUSTRATION ARTIST

Martin Red Bear, M.A.
Oglala Sioux Tribal Member
Professor, Arts and Humanities
Oglala Lakota College
Pine Ridge, SD

PREFACE

Two movie producers had been reading my book, *Mitakuye Oyasin/We are all Related*, with the possibility of making a movie from it. I asked my agent if he thought the idea was viable. He replied that his primary reader, after going through the book, told him it would make an excellent movie once a story line was added. That's when I decided to write this book. My wife, Dorothy, disagreed with the plan because she said I was too young to write an autobiography and that the Dakota/Lakota people might question my motives for writing it. I told her that that was precisely the point: I would want the D/Lakota people to read it and, in fact, for people of any other ethnic origin to read it because if my experiences help at least one D/Lakota person (or any other person) with their problems, then I feel the effort of writing the book will have been justified. By helping others, I help myself.

I had difficulty finding the right words to express my thoughts about an autobiography until I came across the opening lines in *Black Elk Speaks* by John G. Neihardt. Black Elk says, in 1931:

My friend, I am going to tell you the story of my life,...and if it were only the story of my life I think I would not tell it; for what is one man that he should make much of his winters, even when they bend him like a heavy snow? So many other men have lived and shall live that story, to be grass upon the hills.

It is the story of all life that is holy and is good to tell, and of us two-leggeds sharing in it with the four-leggeds and the wings of the air and all green things; for these are children of one mother and their father is one Spirit.

This, then, is not the tale of a great hunter or of a great warrior, or of a great traveler, although I have made much meat in my time and fought for my people both as boy and man, and have gone far and seen strange lands and men. So also have many others done, and better than I.

...So I know that it is a good thing I am going to do; and...no good thing can be done by any man alone,...

Ehanamani

a.k.a.

Allen "Chuck" Ross

CONTENTS

PICTOGRAPHS

INTRODUCTION

In 1851, my ancestors, the Santee Sioux, signed a treaty with the United States government relinquishing 24 million acres in southern Minnesota for $3 million. As part of the payment for the lands, my ancestors were promised farm equipment, farm animals, teachers, and health care. By 1858, 150,000 Europeans had settled in southern Minnesota. My ancestors had relocated to an area 140 miles long and 20 miles wide on both sides of the Minnesota River. In 1858, the government negotiated a new treaty with our Santee people, in which the northern half of this reservation was relinquished, with promises of more money, farm equipment, farm animals, and teachers. In 1861, my ancestors' crops failed and they started moving out into what was their former reservation to hunt. This was against the law, stated the government agents. The agents kept warning my ancestors to stay on the reservation. In 1862, our crops failed again. So we went to the agency for help, and asked when our money from the U.S. government would arrive to help our people through the hard winters. Much of our money had gone to traders in the past because when we needed supplies and goods, we had gone to the traders and bought them on credit. Then when the money came in from the government, the traders would ask the agents to pay the debt. The debt was usually over and above what was actually purchased by our people.

In August of 1862, my Santee ancestors became frustrated because of the lack of help. They went to the government agent and the agent said, "I'll leave it up to the traders." "What do you traders think?" he asked.

One said, "You Sioux could eat grass for all I care."

The traders wouldn't give the people any help, so 400 Santees surrounded the agency and went into the storage cabins and took what they could carry. Still, this was not enough for the entire tribe.

In the meantime, roving bands of our hungry people started to raid the settlers for food. In one incident, they ended up fighting and killing some settlers. With that, our chiefs called a council to decide what to do.

Little Crow, chief of our people, said, "No, no, we must not fight. There are too many; they are too strong." The young men called him a coward.

He replied, "No, I'm not a coward. I have been to Washington, D.C. I rode on the train many days and each morning I woke up and I saw more and more white men. There's no way you will win this war." He continued, "I'm not a coward; I will fight with you and I will die with you."

Thus, a series of seven battles took place. They were started by my Santee ancestors against the U.S. soldiers and surrounding towns. Reinforcements arrived and the last two battles were won by the soldiers who now out-numbered the Santees two to one. The soldiers had cannons, which turned the tide in the battles and brought an end to the eight-week war. This was called a war, not a rebellion, because American Indians were not U.S. citizens until 1924 and were not allowed to vote until 1948.

Four thousand Santees packed up and went west and north into Canada. The remaining Santees, approximately 2,000--most of them women and children, were force-marched to prison at Fort Snelling. They formed a four-mile-long procession in this march. Along the way, the settlers stoned, clubbed, and stabbed the people with pitchforks. After a month of trials, the U.S. government sentenced 303 of the 2,000 to hang. President Lincoln reviewed the trial records and reduced this number to 38. Thirty-eight Santee men were hung on December 26, 1862 in a mass hanging at Mankato, Minnesota. The remaining 1,700 Santees were placed in the compound at Fort Snelling and lived that winter camped out in the cold. My people lacked sufficient firewood and 300 died at Fort Snelling from cold and sickness. The rest of the survivors were loaded onto cattle barges and towed down the Mississippi River and then up the Missouri River to Fort Thompson, South Dakota. There my ancestors remained for three years.

Once again, our crops failed and the people wanted to go home. The government moved them to a reservation in northeastern Nebraska. Many were still homesick and wanted to go back to Minnesota. The federal government finally stated that the Santees could return to their home-lands only if they homesteaded the land like any other U.S. citizen. So twenty-five Santee families did exactly that. They left Nebraska and started for our homeland in Minnesota.

The Homestead Act was passed in the spring of 1862, and much of our Santee homeland was now occupied by settlers who had come mostly from northern Europe. The twenty-five families reached an area along the Big Sioux River that was not homesteaded in what was then called Dakota Territory. C.K. Howard set up a trading post among our people who had homesteaded on the Big Sioux River. The first townsite was named after Charles Flandreau. The Santee of Flandreau organized and became recognized as a tribe under the 1934 Indian Reorganization Act. Today, there are approximately 500 Santees on the Flandreau Santee Sioux Tribal Role; but because of lack of employment on the reservation, fewer than a hundred of us actually live on the Flandreau Santee Sioux Reservation.

RETURN FROM DEATH

My mother was teaching school at Horse Creek Day School on the Rosebud Reservation when she met my father. They were married in December 1939. I was born in October 1940. Since I was the first child, my mother wanted to be at home when she gave birth, so she went to her home in Flandreau, South Dakota. She had gone to the Indian hospital in Pipestone, Minnesota for my birth. Pipestone is known as a place of peace. It was here that tribes gathered to mine the stone from which they made their sacred pipes. If warring tribes met at Pipestone, they would be at peace with one another in that place.

I was born unassisted. When my mother checked in, she was placed in a room. Upon the nurse's return, there I was. I was not given a name until about six weeks after my birth. The family just called me Chaskē, which in Dakota means "the first boy born in the family." That name was Anglicized and I became Chuck. Everybody just called me Chuck except my grandmother and a couple of my aunties who continued to call me Chaskē. Later, I was given the baptismal name of Allen, but everyone continued calling me Chuck.

Born at Pipestone

My father, who had auto mechanics training, could not find work on the Rosebud Reservation. We left Horse Creek Day School in 1942 and went to St. Louis, Missouri where he worked for the McDonnell Douglas Aircraft company, building airplanes for the war. Then with World War II expanding, my father joined the U.S. Army in 1944 and served in the 94th Infantry Division, which was part of Patton's Third Army. He took part in the Battle of the Ardennes. While my father was in the service, my mother, my brother, and I moved to Flandreau where we stayed with my grandparents. I remember my mother had us boys pray for our dad every night before we went to bed.

My grandpa spoke very little English. All I ever remember him speaking was Dakota. He talked to us in Dakota, and we'd answer him in English. When we spoke English to him, he would look at us really hard with disapproval.

My mother had graduated from college with a teaching certificate. When she went to college, she had a very hard time with English. She wanted her boys to have a college education and felt it important that our first language was English. The Dakota we knew was from living on the Flandreau Santee Sioux Reservation and listening to our grandparents.

My father returned from World War II on December 27, 1945. That day always stands out in my memory. We lived in the country on my grandpa's farm. My father was coming down the road. I was the first to see him. He had his uniform on and I thought he was a policeman. I told my grandpa that a policeman was coming. He looked out and saw that it was my father. He quickly told my mother that my dad was coming. She just let out a scream and went running down the road without even putting on her winter coat. Then he told all of us boys to hide, that the policeman was coming to get us. We ran and hid. After my dad came into the house, he wanted to hold us boys, but we were bashful because we did not recognize him. My brother, Hepi, in fact, did not know Dad at all because he was born while my father was overseas.

We stayed with my grandparents until that fall when we got our own land assignment on the reservation at Flandreau and my dad started a farm/ranch. I was five years old that spring before we moved. My father tells a story about how I died and he brought me back to life during that time.

Behind my grandfather's farm is a river called the Big Sioux. Each spring it flooded. That particular spring, my father was working around the barn and I was tagging along behind him when he happened to notice that I was gone. He looked around and couldn't see me anywhere. He followed my footsteps, which headed toward the river. Naturally, he became extremely worried. He jumped on a horse and rode very quickly to the river. He saw my footprints. Evidently, I had followed the calves when they went down to the river. They went into the river; I went into the river.

My father saw where my footprints led into the water of the flooded river. He immediately rode downstream as fast as he could. He found me where a fence was stretched across the river. The barbed wire had caught onto my jacket, and I was hung up on the fence out in the flood. He jumped into the water, swam out to where I was, and pulled me in. I wasn't breathing, so he started artificial respiration. He said a bunch of green water came out of my stomach. He kept on with the artificial respiration and, all of a sudden, I came back to life and started crying.

My grandpa told my dad the traditional Dakota belief was that if someone died and came back to life, that person would be special. I know the Lakotas say if a person dies and comes back to life, that one is going to be spiritual. A concept nowadays called *Walk-in* says that if one dies and comes back to life, an enlightened spirit enters and takes over that person's body; then there are special things that Walk-ins do in their lifetime. I don't feel like I am anyone special, though. I certainly don't feel like a Walk-in.

Return from Death

We received the tribal allotment for our farm/ranch; and since my father was an auto mechanic, he purchased a used tractor. We were one of the first families in the area to get one. It was just a little Ford Ferguson tractor. Everyone else had horses. My father even had me driving that tractor when I was just ten years old. My Grandpa Allen never did get a tractor. He kept horses right up until the day he died.

We lived out in the country with no electricity and no running water. We grew corn and oats. We had alfalfa and would put up hay. We also had pigs, chickens, geese, and ducks. We had to get up very early in the morning and feed the birds; and in the evening we'd feed the pigs. We had about ten milk cows and ten beef cattle. My father had us boys milking cows when we were about ten years old.

I started school at Flandreau Public School. I'll never forget when I was in the first grade, how the kids there made fun of the Indian children. I went home and told my mother what was going on.

She said, "Well you're an Indian too."

I said, "I am?" I didn't realize it. I didn't even see the difference. I thought I was like everybody else. When she said I was an Indian too, I got worried because, as she told me, I didn't want to be teased like the other Indian children and, therefore, didn't want to be Indian.

I remember that I had a difficult time learning to read a clock. It wasn't until later in life that I realized I was a right-brain learner. But in those days, educators simply didn't study different learning styles, and the teacher taught everyone in the same way. I was in third grade and still couldn't tell time. I recall the teacher saying, "OK, Allen, what time is it? The long hand is on twelve and the little hand is on three. What time is it?" I'd look up there at that clock and there was no way I knew what time it was. Now I realize there is a way to teach right-brain children how to tell time. It's called "hands-on education" or "right-brain teaching."

Besides not being able to tell time in school, I also had a difficult time with math. The teachers would explain it to me and explain it to me, but I still couldn't understand. My neighbor, Ralph Hansen, a German, was a math whiz. He'd say, "Come over to my house and I'll help you." So I'd go over to his house. His dad couldn't speak English, only German. I was thankful for the help Ralph gave me with my math problems.

Though math wasn't my strong subject, I held the record in fifth grade for the swing jump. We used to swing as high as we could and then bail out; wherever we landed, we'd make a mark. We'd see who could jump the farthest. I was really proud that I had the school record for the swing jump.

My mother had us boys join the Cub Scouts in Flandreau. We'd go to town for meetings. One time the leaders wanted everybody to bring a show-and-tell item. Since my dad had brought back souvenir coins from different European countries during World War II, I asked if I could take them to the Cub Scout meeting for my show-and-tell. He said I could. I took them, but I forgot them at the meeting and they turned up missing when I went to find them. I caught heck over losing those souvenir coins. Some Cub Scout must have stolen them.

While we were growing up in Flandreau, we were raised in the Episcopal Church. My mother would always volunteer us boys to participate in the Christmas play at the church every year. I would play Joseph because he didn't have to talk; he just stood there. As I got older, I was required to play Santa Claus. I remember my mother used to stuff a pillow under my jacket so I'd look big, fat, and jolly. Of course, I didn't do any talking. The festivities had a master of ceremonies whom the Dakota called an *Eyapaha*, a person who made all the announcements on behalf of others. He would cup his hand over his ear, place it near my mouth, and make believe I talked to him. Then he'd turn around and speak Dakota to all the people at the Christmas party, sometimes telling great jokes and stories as though I had told him what to say.

Back then, people never had a Christmas tree at home. There was only one Christmas tree, and that was at the community building. Everybody took their presents to the community building and all the Indian people would come and sing songs, pass out presents, and have a big Christmas dinner. We used to get one or two gifts. That was it! That was Christmas. Because we couldn't afford to buy any presents, my father made gifts for us. I'll always remember how he carved model airplanes with little propellers. If we blew on them, they would turn. Another time, he carved some stick horses and little guns. That was what our Christmases were like back in the late 40's.

The community center really served the community. All activities for the whole community were celebrated. For instance, if someone had a birthday, the family put on a feed and everyone would come. The cooking stoves were wood-burning ones. The women would have those stoves glowing red-hot in the kitchen. There must have been two or three wood stoves in there, with the women cooking and baking on them. It was always so hot in the kitchen that the women would have sweat running down their faces. The celebrations turned out to be nice, big family affairs. We were all like one big family in those days.

When we went to the community building for these feeds, all the men would sit on one side and all the women and children would sit on the other side. The same way at church: men on one side and women and children on the other side. This is the traditional Dakota way. It wasn't that they were discriminating against anybody; they just realized that everything is in pairs of opposites and that only *Tuŋkašila* (God) was both. In the old days, men had their responsibilities and women had their responsibilities, and working together they'd make the whole. That was the philosophy then.

In the spring of the year right after the river flooded, my grandpa would send us downriver looking for turtle eggs. The turtles would crawl up on the bank, dig a hole, and lay their eggs. Walking along the bank, we could see where the turtles came up. We followed their tracks to where they laid their eggs and then we'd dig them up. The eggs were round and the shells weren't hard yet. They looked like ping-pong balls, but a little bit smaller. We had a little bucket to collect the turtle eggs, and if we could, we'd catch a turtle, too, and bring it back to Grandpa. He really loved turtle soup and turtle eggs. He'd boil most of the eggs, but some of them he'd eat raw. He'd just poke a hole in the egg, put a little salt on it and suck it out.

Once we butchered a turtle. When the turtle is cut into pieces, the heart beats all by itself. Grandpa would say, "Now, if you eat this live turtle heart, you will be a brave warrior."

Well, I tried to eat that turtle heart. I put it in my mouth; it was beating in my mouth; I bit down on it; it would slip out the side of my teeth. I couldn't eat that turtle heart. I remember that one of my cousins took it and just swallowed it.

We would take these live turtle hearts and put them in a jar of water where they started pumping the water around in the jar. That's the first time I got to observe a heart.

Because the turtle is difficult to kill, the Dakota used the reptile as a symbol of long life. When a newborn came into the world, a relative would tie a little turtle pouch, which contained the umbilical cord, around the baby's neck, representing a long life for that infant.

We also butchered cattle, as well as turtles. After butchering, the first parts one would eat were the heart, the liver, and the kidneys. Then Grandma would have us boys down in the river cleaning out the intestines; next, she'd cook them. That'd be the second parts we'd eat. We call that part *tani´ga*. Grandma always said, "Don't get them too clean. Leave some of the hay in there because that's the Indian vitamins." So we'd always leave some of the grass. It kind of added to the flavor.

In addition to running the farm/ranch, my father worked as a part-time mechanic at the Ford garage in Flandreau, and my mother worked as a seamstress at the sewing factory. The factory had the contract to make nightgowns and pajamas for all the government boarding schools in the United States. To help make ends meet, my father had a trapline. He trapped beaver, muskrat, and mink. Sometimes he'd let me follow along and observe how trapping was done. Sometimes I got to help out with some of the stretching and drying of the hides.

Living on the farm/ranch was fun but a lot of work. Dad used to have us driving tractor, plowing the fields, cultivating the corn, cutting hay or something. One spring, we had a few young bulls, and we boys decided we were going to have a rodeo, so we were riding these young bulls. We had taken the saddle and put it on a bull when, all of a sudden, we noticed my dad was coming back from town. We tried to get the saddle off but couldn't. We didn't want to get caught riding those bulls because my dad was very strict and would have really let us have it. Our only choice was to cut that saddle off. Later, when my dad found that the cinch of the saddle had been cut and asked us who did it, none of us would take credit for it. Therefore, he punished me because, as he said, I was the oldest.

My dad had a battery radio when I was a boy. Because he didn't want to run his battery down, he wouldn't let anyone listen to his radio. He reserved the battery for hearing the news and weather report in the morning. Well, in the afternoons when we three boys got back from school, we'd sneak into the room where his radio was and turn it on. We'd listen to "The Lone Ranger" and "Straight Arrow." People had battery-operated radios in those days because, of course, we had no electricity. We had no running water, either, only a pump for household water and an outhouse. We had a wood stove in the kitchen and an oil stove in the living room.

There was a great blizzard in 1949, I recall. The snow-drifts from the barn came off the roof and just leveled off, the snow being twelve feet deep in spots. We had to shovel our way out to the pump where we got our water, then had to pour hot water down it to thaw it out and prime it to get water.

The pheasants put their heads under their wings to endure the blizzard and their wings froze. Therefore, after the blizzard when the pheasants were running around with their heads under their wings, all we had to do was run up and grab them by their legs. We had plenty of pheasant meat right after that blizzard.

During cold weather, we needed to go down by the creek behind our house where we'd chop holes in the ice to water the cows. We'd spread ashes around the ice so the cows wouldn't slip. That winter of '49 when we chopped a hole in the ice, we chopped all the way down to the mud. The creek was frozen all the way through, with ice about three feet thick. We'd find frozen fish in the holes we chopped in the ice and we'd throw them in a bucket to take back to the house. When the fish thawed out, they'd start flopping around. That really amazed me. I thought those frozen fish were dead and, here, they had come back to life.

Blizzard of '49

It was in the spring one year when the creek behind our house was flooded, and my brothers and I were standing on the bank playing and throwing sticks in the water. My brother, Hep, slipped into the flooded creek. We tried to reach him, but he started to drift away. Frightened, I quickly turned and ran into the house to tell my mother. She came dashing out of the house, jumped the fence, and then jumped off a high bank, right into the water beside my brother, who was floating downstream by that time. She grabbed him and pulled him in. We were all relieved. She really surprised me at how fast she could run.

When I was in sixth grade at Flandreau, about six of us boys were playing down along the flooded river and we decided to go swimming. We all jumped in and dared each other to swim across the river. We nearly all swam across and saw that one boy had stayed behind. We hollered at him, daring him to swim across. Finally, he jumped in and started swimming across. He was about halfway when he began going under. He shouted for help, so I jumped into the river and swam out to help him. Just as I got up to him, he grabbed me and we both went underwater. I would barely get free and come up for a breath of air and he'd grab me again. And under we'd go. This happened twice. Then the third time I came up, I saw some grapevines hanging in the water and grabbed onto them. As soon as I grasped the vines, my friend clutched onto me, climbed up my body and right up those grapevines. He was just hanging up there. I swam to shore and the others boys and I got a log that we floated out there to where I had been. We tried to get our friend to drop down onto the log. Well he wouldn't come down. After a lot of coaxing, we got him down onto the log. He hung on and we paddled him to shore. He was a childhood friend named Fred Smith. We saved his life that day.

While we were on the farm, we had large gardens every year. We spent a lot of time planting and maintaining our garden and then we'd harvest it. I enjoy being in a garden. It gives off a certain smell that really makes me feel good.

I can never remember not having food. We had year-round produce from the garden because my mom always canned. Besides the quantity of vegetables in storage, we also had the beef cattle. My mother customarily gave thanks for our food at mealtime. She said long ago the Indians prayed before they planted or went hunting. Nowadays we pray at mealtime.

Whenever it was harvest time at the farm, all the neighbors would help each other. I remember we used to have threshing machine parties. All the neighbors would come and help with the threshing, and the women all cooked and fed everybody. Then we'd all move on to the next farm and help the neighbor with his threshing. Once when we were threshing out at my grandpa's place, the men would cut the oats and put them into little bundles. We'd stand the bundles up so they wouldn't rot. There'd be all these shocks of oats standing up in the field. We came with wagons, loaded the shocks, and then hauled them to the threshing machine, where they were thrown into the machine to separate the stalk from the grain. One time we had worked late. The sun had gone down and there was one load left. I happened to be driving. Because it was the last load of oat shocks, the others told me to hurry up before it got completely dark. I went ahead and put the tractor in third gear and took off. Well, I hit a bump and caused an old wooden wheel we had on the hay rack to break apart, and the whole wagon tipped over. People drove out there with their cars to shine the headlights on the accident. They had to bring another hay rack and we reloaded all those shocks to take to the threshing machine. That's the way it was in the old days: people really helped one another. That's how everyone got along.

An early winter morning one day when we were living on the farm, we were having breakfast when my mother suddenly said, "There's a white owl sitting in the tree outside." She made all of us boys, Pānk, Hep, Jim Bill and myself, gather around to see the white owl. (Three of us boys, by the way, had gotten our nicknames from our childhood Dakota names: "Chuck" from "Chaskē;" "Pānk" from "Hepāna," meaning "second boy;" and "Hep" from "Hepi," meaning "third boy.") She told us that, according to traditional Dakota belief, it is a sign of good luck to see a white owl. That's why she wanted all of us to see the white owl. That event has really stuck in my mind, that all four of us boys saw that white owl.

White Owl, "Good Luck"

One fall Dad and I were picking corn with our corn picker. I was in the wagon in the back of the picker where the corn ears would fall. I leveled out the corn so more ears could be loaded into the wagon. This was when corn pickers first came out and all the bugs hadn't been worked out of them yet. The machine would get clogged up every once in awhile; when that happened, my dad would stop and clean it out. Then we'd go on. Well, one time when the picker clogged up, I noticed that my dad was cleaning it out and, all of a sudden, he began pulling on his hand until it came free. As a result of that accident, my dad lost three fingers and part of a fourth, so the neighbors had to come and finish picking corn for us. After that, my dad and mother decided to give up farming and go on relocation.

What had happened, I found out later, was that Dad's hand had gotten caught in the husking rollers of the corn picker, and he had pulled it out. If he hadn't done that, he would have lost his hand and maybe his whole arm. He had on a silver ring that he had made from a silver dollar, and that's what had temporarily stopped his hand from going into the rollers all the way. The pause gave him time to pull his hand out.

RELOCATION

The summer after my dad's accident, we went to California looking for work. We spent a couple of months there with relatives, then moved on to Wichita, Kansas. My folks couldn't find anything there either. We ended up in St. Louis, Missouri. It was late September when my dad found a job at McDonnell Aircraft Company, where he had worked right before the war. Thus, we relocated to St. Louis. We stayed there for the rest of the year, but the weather was so humid that my dad couldn't stand it. Besides, my mother couldn't find a decent job. Even though she had a degree in education, she couldn't get a teaching job and ended up working as a waitress in a cafe. We lived in a trailer court where there were a lot of hillbillies who always called us dirty Indians. We'd end up fighting with them. My dad told me never to start a fight, but if forced into one, not to run from it. We stayed there only seven months, then finally decided to move back to South Dakota.

We left St. Louis right at the end of school that year and went to the Rosebud Reservation in South Dakota where my father's parents lived. Their community was Oak Creek. My dad left us there with my grandparents while he and my mother looked for work elsewhere in the state. We boys played with our cousins who lived there at Oak Creek. They had a lot of horses that we would all get on and ride up and down the creek. We really had a good time that summer. I have many pleasant memories of playing there.

There were some high hills about five miles behind my grandpa's house. We were up there playing one time and found some beads lying on the ground. We started digging in the dirt and found coins and moccasins. That really excited us! We gathered them up, rode down to Grandpa's house and told him about what we had found. He said, "That's an old burial site. You boys should just leave it alone." He took all the things we had found back up there to rebury them.

I learned a lot from my grandpa. He started telling us about the old ways and how the people used to place their relative who had died on scaffolds on top of the hills where we had found the artifacts. He said it took four seasons for the spirit to go on. Everything--the dead and their belongings--had to be left right there during that time.

I told my father about my grandpa telling us of the traditional ways. My father, in turn, told me a story. He said, "Yes, your grandpa believes in traditional ways. I remember one time one of my great-uncles had gotten lost in a blizzard and never returned home. After the blizzard, Grandpa looked for him and looked for him but couldn't find him, so he went to a Yuwipi ceremony that Old Man Horn Chips performed."

The spirits said, in the ceremony, that my father's great-uncle had died in the blizzard, but they told him where his relative could be found. "There were two buttes right on the west side of Oak Creek," my dad continued, "and at the bottom of the second butte is where the spirits told us we would be able to find my great-uncle. Grandpa went there and, sure enough, he found him." The relatives then had a funeral for him.

Grandpa Ross also told us that Oak Creek (called O'Kreek nowadays) was the center of reservation activity until it burned down. Then the center moved to Mission, South Dakota.

My Grandma Ross was an herbalist. She made teas for a number of different ailments. I remember there was kind of a joke with us boys: when you go to Grandma Ross' house, don't get sick because she's going to make you drink one of her herb teas. Some of them were really bitter. That's why when we went to her house, we made an extra effort to stay healthy. She had a large selection of herbs and it was one of her gifts to help others.

My father found a job in Rapid City. When he got to the site, the prospective employer discovered he was an Indian and told him the job was filled. My folks really felt bad about it and were unable to find work anywhere in Rapid City. They stopped at Pine Ridge on the way back to Rosebud, where my aunt and uncle who lived there told my mother that Pine Ridge Boarding School was looking for teachers.   She applied for a job and got one teaching primary. (Primary was pre-kindergarten then, not grades one through three as it is now.)   In those days, all the kids attending the school were Lakota speakers only.   At the primary level, the goal was to teach the students English, numbers, and colors--the basics--so they could be prepared for kindergarten.   My mother actually taught bilingual education fifty-five years ago!   It wasn't called bilingual education then; it was just teaching English.   One of the major ways she taught was with songs, using the same songs in both Lakota and English.   It really worked.   Today, educators call this whole-brain teaching.

My father had to wait a little bit longer before he could find a job, but he did eventually get a job at the government garage. In the meantime, while waiting to get a job, he went hunting. We used to eat a lot of wild game when my parents didn't have jobs: deer, antelope, grouse, pheasant, rabbits.

That year we moved to the Oglala Community School at Pine Ridge, South Dakota.   We lived in a one-bedroom government apartment; that's all that was available.   We boys had to sleep downstairs in a makeshift bedroom.

I entered the seventh grade there in Pine Ridge.   We boys became what everyone called BIA (Bureau of Indian Affairs) brats.   It was a boarding school for students on the Pine Ridge Reservation, where local students were called day students.   We didn't stay at the school like the boarding students did.   I hung out with the boys in the neighborhood: the Red Clouds, the Hands, Red Stars, Eagle Elks, Tyons,

Mosseaus, and we became very cliquish. Our good friendships developed because we day-school students were discriminated against by the boarding school kids. We put up with name-calling and being tripped and shoved by the boarding students.

I learned how to play football and how to run track from the older BIA brats. Owen Eagle Elk and Elmer Red Star were particularly good football players who taught me much about football and track.

Our house was right at the edge of campus and Old Man Red Cloud, the son of the original Chief Red Cloud, used to walk right by our house every day as he went into town. He came right through our yard, and sometimes he'd stop and say hello and would visit with the folks, then go on. He never spoke English when he visited, only Lakota.

We used to play up and down White Clay Creek, which was below the school. In the winter time we'd play hockey on it. We made a little hockey field and set up goals. I remember that we'd get a can and crunch it for our puck. And we'd get diamond willow branches to make hockey sticks. Sometimes we'd play down there all day long and wouldn't even go home at noon because we were having so much fun.

As I got older, I had a trapping line up and down the creek. I made some traps out of ropes. One time I bent a tree over near the creek and made a little snare with a rope. I used some sardines for bait. The next morning I was checking out my trap line when I heard a dog howling. As I got closer to my snare, I saw that a dog was hanging by his front legs in the air. I thought when I set the trap that I was going to get a rabbit or a coyote, but I ended up getting a dog.

White Clay Creek emptied into White Clay Dam. In the fall, many ducks and geese came there, providing us brothers with good hunting in that area in the winter. One time the north wind blew, causing the ducks to huddle along the bank on the north edge. We sneaked up on some of them and shot about a dozen ducks. But the wind blew them away from the shore. We decided to walk around on the other side of the dam and pick up our birds as soon as the wind blew them in. We did just that. By the time we got to the other side of the dam, nightfall was coming, it was growing dark and starting to snow. All of a sudden as we began walking back around the dam, it got completely dark and a big blizzard came up. We couldn't see and we got lost. We didn't know where we were. I recalled what my dad had said: "If you get lost in a blizzard, follow the fence line." As soon as we found a fence line, we followed it. We didn't even know were it was going to lead us, but it dropped down into a little ravine where we huddled up in a snowbank. It was so cozy there we thought about going to sleep. My brother, Pānk, did fall asleep.

Finally, I said, "Let's get out of here. We'd better keep on going." So we got up and continued to follow the fence line. It led us right to the horse barn at Oglala Community School. Then I knew where we were, comprehending that we had made it home. Later I learned that if we had gone to sleep, we might not have awakened.

The Oglala Community School had school gardens. We students took care of them while they grew and then did the harvesting. We had what they called agriculture classes. Everybody had to take Agriculture in those days. In the fall, when everybody came back to school, the agriculture classes had to go out and harvest the gardens. There were potatoes, tomatoes, carrots, and cucumbers that we'd pick and take to a giant underground cellar. We called it a spud cellar where the school stored staples. We ate these vegetables as part of our school meals. The school also had dairy barns with a large herd of milk cows. We lived right next to a dairy barn and each morning at 5:00 a.m., we could hear the milk cans clanging. In those times, hardly any food was wasted at mealtime.

There at Oglala Community School, I joined the band. I played snare drums, but since there was just two sets of snares and more than two drummers, we had to take turns. The band leader's name was Mr. Rider, a trumpet player. Only about five or six boys and probably about ten girls were in the band. We learned about five or six songs; then Mr. Rider would take us on a trip to all the district day schools out on the reservation where we had to play little concerts. We'd drive into the schoolyard, get out of the bus, and play for the students right there in the schoolyard. Day schools didn't have large auditoriums where everyone could gather. My recollection is that when all the kids gathered around to hear us perform, their eyes would be just big watching us. When we'd play at these concerts, I never got to play the drums because only the older boys were allowed to play them. I had to play the cymbals instead. I remember that when we gave a concert at Oglala School in Pine Ridge, Mr. Rider blew his horn the loudest of anyone in the band. We sounded like a one-horn band!

While living at Oglala Community School, my brothers and I used to go deer hunting. For many years, my dad would take us hunting. He'd let us off and say, "I'll drive around to the other side of the canyon and wait for you." I didn't realize it then, but he was using us kind of like bird dogs. He'd drive around to the other end and we'd go tromping through the canyon and spook out all the deer to him, waiting there by the canyon's end. Other times he'd just take us out and leave us, then come back and get us at sunset. He said that if we ever got lost, we should go to the highest hill and look around to get our bearings.

Well, one time when we were out hunting, I shot a deer and just wounded it. It was running on three legs. I was chasing it as fast as I could, not following my father's advice. He had told me, "If you ever wound a deer, just sit down, wait a half hour and it will go over the hill and sit down. If you chase it, it will just keep running." Well, I was chasing the deer, without even paying any attention to where I was running. I couldn't catch him, so I began tracking him. I saw where he had jumped over a fence and had fallen down. A puddle of blood was there, which means he must have lain there for a while and then on he went. I was intensely following the tracks.

Eventually, it started getting dark. I looked around and became aware that I didn't know where I was. I had been so busy chasing the deer that I didn't notice where I was going and got lost. I took my dad's advice and went to the highest

30

hill and started looking around to get my bearings. I could see Slim Buttes. I thought I had my bearings, so I started walking. I looked in another direction and said to myself, "Wait a minute; there's Slim Buttes over there." Every butte I looked at looked like Slim Buttes. I went to the next highest hill. By this time, it was getting very dark. I became frightened. There were no electric lights, of course, to brighten the darkness. I'll always remember how scared I was out there in the dark. When I was walking down a canyon and heard a noise, I turned around and shot my gun right into the darkness. To this day, I don't know what was out there. Maybe it was a cow or horse or some other animal. I was just 13 years old at the time.

Finally, though, I saw a light from a log cabin way off in the distance and started walking toward it. I got halfway to the light and it went out. I just kept going in that direction and pretty soon when dogs started barking, I knew I was close to something. I went up to the log cabin, which turned out to be Barney Makes Shine's mother's place. Then I knew where I was. I had shot a couple of rabbits that day, and I gave them to Mrs. Makes Shine and took off down the road for home.

The staff at Oglala Community School set aside one day out of the year for a track and field day. They'd bring in all the kids from all the day schools to participate. Because I liked track and field, I went to this event. We students from Oglala Community School didn't get to take part, though, just the day-school students from the reservation district schools. When I was in the eighth grade, a girl from Kyle

31

was winning all the races, winning the high jump and the broad jump at the field day. I'll always remember that because, years later, she and I became husband and wife.

While in the eighth grade at Oglala Community School, disaster struck for me. What I mean is that I started drinking alcohol. The first time I drank beer, I had two cans and got drunk. My drinking started from peer pressure. My buddies said, "Come on, let's go." We hitchhiked to White Clay and got a six-pack of beer. We each had two cans. I didn't realize it at the time--I thought it was just having fun--but that was the start of a long disastrous road for me, the beginning of alcoholism. I was only thirteen years old at the time.

BISHOP HARE SCHOOL

Our one-bedroom house at Oglala Community School where we boys slept in the basement had steam heat and it was really humid down there. I had tremendous sinus problems and the doctor said that I shouldn't stay in the basement. That's one of the reasons the folks decided to send us boys to Bishop Hare School. The other reason was that my dad is from the Rosebud Reservation where Bishop Hare School was located, and he wanted us to go to school on his home reservation. Bishop Hare School was a boarding home for Episcopalian Indian boys. The boys stayed at the home and attended Todd County Public High School. My brother, Pānk, and I applied to and were accepted at Bishop Hare School. I was a ninth grader and Pānk was an eighth grader. Bishop Hare School was located about a quarter of a mile from town and we had to walk to school in all types of weather--rain, snow, you name it. It was quite an experience.

Bishop Hare School did our laundry for us, but all of our clothes had to be marked with our names on them. In those days we used India ink to mark our clothing. One boy's clothes always ended up missing, even with his name on them. Somebody was taking his clothes. Finally he just put a big black X on his shorts and t-shirts. That way, if he saw his black X walking around, he knew those were his shorts.

Bishop Hare School Boy

I had a lot of memorable experiences at the Bishop Hare School. Since it was a church school, we had to go to church. We had evening prayer every day and Holy Communion on Wednesday and Sunday. The boys were required to take turns leading the evening prayer. We went to church three times on Sunday.

One of my more enjoyable experiences there occurred when I was a ninth grader. I was making a model paddle-wheel riverboat and needed a motor to run the paddle-wheel. I had noticed the cook's clock in the kitchen and borrowed it. Well, let's be honest--I stole the clock. I took the motor for my boat and put her clock back on the shelf, but she didn't know the motor was missing until later. I had my boat out at the dam behind the school. It was working really well and I wanted to show it off. I told some of the older boys about it. When they saw my paddle-wheel boat chugging along the shore, they got rocks and bombarded it.

Another time I had made a steam turbine engine. I hooked it onto the radiator and when I turned on the radiator, the steam would turn that little turbine motor. I would hook up little pulleys and operate my motor. One morning when I left for school, I forgot to take my motor off the radiator. The head of the school, Mr. John Artichoker, said he heard this rattling upstairs; he went to investigate and saw this contraption hooked onto the radiator. Steam was blowing out the turbine engine, and it was spinning as fast as it could, making the entire radiator shake. He thought, "What in the world is this?" That evening, he gave us boys a lecture about steam escaping from the radiators. He complained about my steam engine, but I could tell he really liked my invention.

I was always doing little things like that. Once I set a booby trap. I hung up a punching bag on the garage door and rigged it so that when someone opened the door, the bag would drop down and hit the person in the chest. Mr. Artichoker came walking through the door and that punching bag hit him right square in the chest. Because he was a big man, it didn't knock him down, but it did make him stagger backwards. He got a chuckle out of that, but he wanted to know who had set the trap. I don't think we ever told him who did it. No one would ever own up to the deed.

In the wintertime we played a modified version of basketball in the basement of our dormitory. We'd make little goals out of coat hangers and weave a net onto them. Then we'd use a tennis ball for a basketball. That was one of our main activities in the wintertime. We set up games and had tournaments, a natural extension of high school basketball. In my sophomore year at Todd County High School, I played football, basketball, and track, lettering in all the sports.

Also in the wintertime at Hare School, I had a trapping line. I was able to borrow some of my dad's old traps that he had used. I caught beaver, muskrat, and mink. I recalled that my dad had said, "Before you set up your trapping line, smoke your traps before you set them." This was to get rid of my scent on the traps. He also advised, "When you check your traps, you don't go right up to them; you look from a distance. Maybe from across the creek. If you get too close, you'll leave your smell there and the animals won't come around." I used ice skates and skated up the creek to check my lines. One time when I had caught some beaver, I dried the hides and took them in to sell, but the man wouldn't buy them. He said they needed to be stretched in the round. So I had to learn the hard way by stretching them all over again.

The muskrats I dried by getting a shingle and shaping the front of it to a point. Then I'd pull the hide over with the hair down next to the shingle. Soon the shingles started disappearing off the garage. As in the steam engine incident, John Artichoker wanted to know what was happening, where all the shingles were going. I didn't tell him I was using them to dry my muskrat hides. At that time, I used to get about $.50 for rabbit, $1.00 for muskrat hide, and $5.00 for beaver hides. Mink hides brought about $20.00. That was a lot of money in those days.

Trapper

We had gone back to Pine Ridge for Thanksgiving vacation one year and were out hunting deer in the Slim Buttes area. We were walking way out in the middle of nowhere and, all of a sudden, I saw human footprints in the dirt. The tracks went down the road in front of us. Later, they disappeared. Then as we were sitting up on a hill, I noticed something blue down below in the grass. As I got closer, I saw it was a man lying there. (The blue color I had seen was part of his clothing.) We really got scared and ran. When Dad came to pick us up, we told him about it and he got the police, who went out there and found the man. He had been murdered. There are many unsolved murders on the reservation, and they are usually alcohol-related. I'll never forget finding that man. At first, I thought maybe when we were hunting, we had accidentally shot him, but the police said he had been stabbed to death.

In the summer months we'd go back to Pine Ridge. I remember the first summer after attending Hare School, we had a job working on the Hinn Ranch south of Rushville, Nebraska. We cut and stacked hay for Mr. Hinn. He'd bring us to town on Saturday nights. On weekdays, we'd get up with the chickens. Early-morning chores included feeding and watering the sheep and chickens. The rancher worked us sun-up to sundown. But he really fed us well. For breakfast we could get all the pancakes and eggs we wanted, and at noon his wife would bring out a meal almost like a Thanksgiving dinner. We could eat as much chicken and mashed potatoes and biscuits as we wanted. The pay wasn't worth a darn, though, only about $6.00 a day plus room and board. That's what we earned for pitching hay.

One summer I had gotten a job working for the Episcopal Church in the Black Hills. A man had given a lot of land to the church, but before the deed was to be turned over, he wanted to prospect for gold on his property one last time. There was a man from the Homestake Gold Mine who was to do the last explorations for gold. Well, my brother, Pānk, and I and a couple of other friends worked with this man, looking for gold. We'd dig six-foot deep holes in the ground with an iron tamper and place them about four feet apart: two holes, then one hole in between and below the first two, then two more holes below that center one. The arrangement of the holes looked like a five on a dice. Then the Homestake man would get a stick of dynamite, slice the side open and put a blasting cap in with the fuse, drop it down in the hole, then put two more sticks of dynamite on top of that. All the holes had fuses sticking out at the top. Next, the man would send us down into the canyon to stop all the traffic. What I mean by traffic was animals because there were no roads out there. Then he'd calmly light the fuses with his cigarette and walk uphill. The blast blew a big hole in the side of the hills. He'd take samples of the earth in to see if there were any gold deposits.

One weekend, with nothing to do, we were messing around, digging in an old mine shaft. The Hills were full of old mine shafts where people had dug, prospecting for gold. We had gone into one of the old mine shafts where I began to dig. I had gotten pretty far in there when I suddenly broke through into something. I lay down on the ground and reached my hand into the hole I had made. I was excited and thought maybe I had found a gold mine. But as I was lying there, reaching into the hole, something told me to get up. Just as I stood up, the old shaft caved in and pinned me from the chest on down. A big wall of dirt had fallen on me. I thought I could just push it aside and crawl out but to my surprise, I couldn't move. One arm was pinned, the other one free. It took my brother and our friends about a half-hour to get me out of the dirt. I was really thankful that I wasn't still lying on the ground when that wall caved in.

My junior year in high school, as was the custom, the Hare School boys were invited to have a dinner and dance social with the St. Mary's girls, St. Mary's School being an Episcopalian Indian girls' school. Mr. Artichoker put us in the back of a pick-up and took us to Springfield, S.D., a little over 100 miles away. We went there dressed up to go to dinner with the girls. I remember everybody being afraid to eat, all of us watching our manners. They served us fried chicken, potato chips, and corn. Everybody was trying to cut their chicken with a knife and fork. Finally, one of the boys said, "Hands were made before forks," and he picked up his chicken and started eating. All the other boys picked up their chicken and started eating with their hands. But the girls were still dainty, trying to cut their chicken with their knives and forks. Boy, that was a miserable time eating at those social dinners!

Afterwards, at the dance, which was a record hop, the boys wouldn't dance. They just stood around and looked nice. The girls were the only ones dancing. They danced with each other. At these church socials, the lights had to be on. Finally, though, the chaperons at this dance agreed to turn the lights low. Then everybody rushed out onto the floor and danced.

Where Todd County High School was built, you had to go across a little creek to get to the gym. It was about 300 yards away from the school. School was dismissed at 3:30 for basketball practice and whoever was first to the gym got the new basketballs to practice with. Everybody used to race to see who would be the first one to the gym. Well, the white boys had cars and they'd all come out and jump in their cars and drive to the gym. All of us Indian boys were on foot, so we'd have to run fast. I was one of the lucky ones, always getting to the gym among the first ones so I could practice with a new basketball. That really didn't help us too much in deciding who got to play. One white boy would be on the team when there'd be five or six Indian players on the bench who were better than that white boy. Finally, we protested. We went to the coach and asked about the discrepancy. He said, "Well, that's what the school board wants. They want a white boy on the team." That was really an eye opener for us! It was an all-white school board, even though the school was over 50% Indian. White people obviously ran the school.

In the summer months after my junior year, I went to work at Buckingham Wood Products in Rapid City, South Dakota, a pre-fabricated housing company. I loaded pre-fab houses onto semi-trucks and the drivers hauled them out to housing projects. The next year, I worked for them again and they gave me a little promotion. In those days, Indians were generally just laborers, but my second year there, Vern Potts, the foreman, let me drive the forklift and gave me some responsibilities, which I enjoyed. The pay was $1.25 an hour, a lot of money at that time.

During the summer months, I used to party on weekends. I got a paycheck every week and sometimes I'd spend the whole check on partying. I finally decided to buy some school clothes right away when I got paid so I wouldn't party up all my money.

In my senior year, I returned to Bishop Hare School a couple weeks early for football practice. The first week I was back, I went out partying and John Artichoker, the headmaster, told me, "We can't have that. We have rules here. There's no drinking allowed in school." He kicked me out of Hare School and I called my folks to come get me. They came and talked to Mr. Artichoker, staying in the office for over an hour. Finally, he called me in and said, "OK, you can stay, but you're going to be on probation." I was on probation all fall semester of my senior year. I also had to work in the kitchen that whole semester. But we did have a good football season. We lost only one game, our first one, by just one point. Later on, we won games with two teams that had beaten the team that beat us in that first game. We felt, therefore, that we were a better team than they were.

I lucked out and made captain of the football team that year. During Homecoming, I was asked to make a speech at the bonfire pep rally. The cheerleaders said, "Now we'll hear a speech from Captain Chuck Ross."

I was so bashful that I couldn't talk. I took one step out into the middle of the arena and all I said was, "I hope we win. Thank you." (Nowadays, it's said that if Chuck Ross starts talking, you can't get him to shut up.)

We had exceptionally fast runners on our football team. The year before, we had won the half-mile relay race in the state meet. We had five boys who could run the 100-yard dash in 10.4 seconds and under. Four of them were in the backfield of our football team, making us one of the fastest backfields in the state of South Dakota, if not *the* fastest.

My senior year, though, we were moved up into the Class A division because of the rise in our high school enrollment. We complained that within a month, there'd be ten kids dropping out of school and we wouldn't truly be Class A. The principal said, "No, no, we're going to stay Class A. It will be good practice for you boys." We ended up in Class A competition and took third place in the state in the half-mile relay. Since our time was faster than the Class B record, we really felt like we had been cheated out of the Class B record in the half-mile relay. The principal was a white man whom we felt was jealous, not wanting us to have the state record.

Our relay team consisted of my brother, Pānk, Roy Red Shirt, Percy Byrnes and myself. Though I was on the team, my specialties were the high jump and running the hurdles.

Hurdler

When I graduated, many of the students were showered with gifts. I didn't get many gifts--maybe one or two, but it didn't bother me. My mother said to me, "This is not the end of the line for you. It's just the beginning. You're going to college. For many of these students, they're finished with their education and that's probably why they're getting a lot of gifts, but you're going to go on to college."

SERPENT VISION

I worked in Rapid City in the summer months. When my brother, Pānk, and I first went there, we got living quarters in a motel. It was a nice room and the folks were with us when we checked in. A week later, the motel people moved us out of the motel room and put us in a barn-looking shed out behind the motel. The door to this building had a Dutch door on it that made it look like a barn. When my folks came up to visit a couple weeks later, my dad saw what had happened and he really got angry. He took us out of there and found an apartment where we could stay for the summer while we worked.

My brother, Hep, had a job working at Sitting Bull Cave. Pānk and I went to see him once, and he told us about the old lady who owned the cave. She had given him a paper with stories to memorize, which he had to tell the tourists. Concrete had been poured at the entrance of the cave and somebody had stepped in it when it was wet. It hardened, of course, and the story Hep was supposed to tell the tourists was that this was Sitting Bull's footprint which was left there. My brother said that the employees also had to haul water down to the bottom of the cave to fill a small hole.

Then they went out and seined minnows to put in the little pool of water. Hep was required to tell the tourists that this was an underground river and that the fish were full-grown, but their growth had been stunted and they were totally blind, both conditions brought about by the darkness of the cave. The tourists really enjoyed these stories. Hep wore a turkey feather war bonnet and a fringed buckskin jacket. He and his buddy, Ed Codier, made more money on tips than they did in salary. The old lady found out they were making a lot of money on tips and she started taking their tips. When Dad learned about the situation, he talked to her about it. After that, she left the boys' tips alone.

In the summer months my brother, Pānk, Dick Menzie, Schop Mousseau, and I, used to go to various rodeos as amateur participants. We had gone to a rodeo at Interior one weekend. Back then, there were no night rodeos; when it got dark, the rodeo was over. A lot of drinking went on at rodeos. I guess the idea was that, in order to be a rodeo rider, you had to be a big tough man, and only big tough men could drink. Well, we hung around the rodeo for a little bit. It got dark, and we decided we'd better get back to Rapid City where we worked.

We left. I was driving as we traveled through the Badlands, headed toward Wall, South Dakota. All the roads were gravel at that time and were really winding. We came around a corner and there was a telephone pole lying in the road. I hit the brakes and we bumped over the pole. No sooner had we run over it, than I realized it wasn't a telephone pole but a giant snake. Chills went right up my backbone. (kundalini?) I hollered at the guys, who were asleep, and told them what I had seen. We turned around and, with the car headlights on, we began looking for the snake. We were too scared to get out of the car. We looked for the snake, but it was gone. I didn't tell anybody that story for a long time because I didn't think anyone would believe me. Even today I wonder if that was an actual snake or if it was a vision. I know that the psychologist, C.G. Jung, said if one has a dream or a vision about a serpent, it symbolizes transcendence. That is, the incident is a symbol for being able to communicate with the unconscious mind. I wondered if the serpent was a vision. Even though we bumped over that snake and I felt it, to this day, I still don't know if it was a vision or a real snake.

Serpent Vision

As mentioned previously, I used to buy my school clothes each payday. I bought a lot of western shirts and wranglers. When I went to college, my mother said, "You're going to have to dress up to go to college. That's proper." I did buy a few things that I thought were clothes one should wear at college. But once I got to the University of South Dakota, everybody kind of looked at me with smirks on their faces, as if to say, "What are you doing here?" I had bought some V-neck shirts (they were popular then) and bright-colored trousers. Because of the smirks, I just took them off and put my wranglers and boots back on and that's how I went to school.

Later in my life, while studying the psychic readings of Edgar Cayce, I learned that mankind was to experience forty years of change, to begin in 1958. I wondered if my attitude about changing the dress code for college attendance had a connection to this prophecy. It had occurred in 1958!

Fewer than ten Indian students attended school at the University of South Dakota when I first went there. The administration put the Indian students, foreign students, and the black jocks (black students who were on athletic scholarships) in one wing of the dorm. We were segregated at that time.

The dining room at the dorm was closed on Sundays. We'd save money for Sunday meals and sometimes had only one meal that day. An ROTC sergeant named Tinker had a chili diner downtown where he'd serve a big bowl of chili and crackers for $1.00. I would always save $1.00 and on Sundays, I'd wait until I couldn't stand the hunger pains any longer and then I'd go eat a big bowl of chili to hold me over till breakfast Monday morning. Sgt. Tinker was from Oklahoma and claimed to be part Indian. He treated me pretty well.

I wasn't used to classes as large as at the University of South Dakota where there could be 100 students in a class. It was like I was just a number. I really didn't do well in my schoolwork and I took some courses that I thought would be easy, trying to raise my grade point average. A Lakota there named Oscar Howe was an art professor and was internationally known as an artist. I took an art course under him, thinking I would get an easy "A" to help raise my overall average. But instead, he not only expected me to be as good as he, but he also expected extra work from me. I worked my tail off and all I got was a "C."

I had gone out for track in college. The track coach, Mr. Dan Lennon, had approached me at the state high school track meet and asked me to come to USD (University of South Dakota) and he'd give me a scholarship. I agreed. But when I got there, he found out that I had a BIA scholarship, so he dropped the track scholarship but still wanted me to come out for track. I remember how he stereotyped me. Most Indians are excellent distance runners, and he concluded that because I was Indian, I would be good in distance running. He practically forced me to go out for cross-country. The events I ran were hurdles, broad jump, and the quarter-mile. I could never run distance races. When I ran track for the University of South Dakota, I was what they called a point getter. I just placed fourth or fifth, sometimes third in the events. Anybody knows when you have a track team, it's nice to have winners, but if you don't have depth, then a lot of times you're not able to win the track meet. I added depth to the track team by being a point getter. I did take one first place during my university stint, though--in the broad jump. It's the only first place I ever took in college. I jumped 22 feet and 3 inches to win the broad jump. I know that's not very far, but I'm really proud of the jump anyway.

There were about five or six of us Indian boys at USD, and we dressed western. A couple of boys from Sioux City, Iowa named Bob and Bill Landis also dressed western, and they were really interested in starting a rodeo club. They asked us if we were interested. We said, "Sure." We put out advertisements and got about thirty girls and only about ten boys to start our rodeo club. Then we decided we needed to put on a rodeo. Our first step was to build an arena. We built some chutes from scratch, spending whole weekends working on them and on the rodeo arena itself. Then we contacted Bob Burnes from Cherokee, Iowa. He was to bring livestock for the rodeo. He brought a truckload of horses to test our chutes. He ran them into the chutes and they just tore our structures apart.

He said, "I'm sorry, boys. I can't bring my animals up here. They'll get hurt in these chutes." We got our heads together and decided to rebuild the chutes. I didn't even go to class, taking time off from school to work on rebuilding the chutes. We rebuilt everything and then phoned Bob Burnes again.

He came back, took one look at the chutes, and said, "OK, I'll help you guys put on your rodeo." And we did--the first one at the University of South Dakota. One of our Lakota boys, Dick Menzie, won the bull riding that year. Our university rodeo club was really proud of him.

We'd go around to different college rodeos in the rodeo circuit. I rode in the bareback riding contest in Fargo, North Dakota and got hurt. The horse I rode was so big, I said to the chute boss, "Are you sure this is bareback or is it saddle bronc?"

He said, "No, this is bareback." Boy, it sure was a big horse! Well, I tore a muscle in my leg during my ride, which ended my college track and rodeo career.

The University of South Dakota was at Vermillion, which was about thirty miles from Yankton. One weekend two or three of us Indian students had gone bar hopping in Yankton. When we went into a bar in south Yankton, the bartender said, "We don't serve Indians in here." We left and when we got back to Vermillion, we told the track jocks, who were also football players, what had transpired.

They said, "Well, we'll go with you. We'll show those guys." We told them no, just to forget the matter, because we didn't want any trouble with those people.

Because of my low grades, I decided to transfer to a smaller college. I selected Black Hills State College in Spearfish because some friends I knew were going to school there. Not only that, but Black Hills State had about fifty Indian students and it was closer to home. The University of South Dakota was about 300 miles from home and I'd gotten lonesome. When I first went to Black Hills, I roomed with a fellow from India. He would say to me, "You're not an Indian. I'm the real Indian." I got tired of him reminding me of this. One weekend I went out and had one too many beers.

When I came back to our room, I told him, "Get out of bed, *real Indian*, get out of bed and dance. If you are a real Indian, I want to see you dance." Well, needless to say, he left. The next day the "real Indian" moved out. He was still in college. He just moved out of my room.

When my brother, Pānk, and I first went to Black Hills State College, we tried out for football. The coach, I think, was prejudiced, because he never really gave us a chance. He'd just use us for blocking practice. So we quit football. At Homecoming that year, the Indian Club decided to enter a float in the parade. We started building it in the afternoon, and later on in the evening, someone said, "Let's get some beer." We got a case of beer, started drinking, and did not complete the float that day.

The next morning we were rushing around, trying to complete the float in time for the parade. We did not finish decorating it but instead, we got some star quilts and covered the hood of the truck and the doors with them. Doug White Bull said, "Let's draw straws to see who's going to drive it because nobody wants to." Wilbur Smith ended up the driver. We went downtown to watch the parade. When our float came into view, we were eager to see it. It was a stork with a diaper in its bill and a football in the diaper. Halfway through the parade, one of the wings fell off the stork and then, right when it got in front of us, the stork's bill broke, causing the diaper to fall and the football to go bouncing down the street. We really got embarrassed and tried to hide because people knew that was our float.

While attending college at Black Hills State, my brother, Pānk, had gone out for track. At one track meet, he ran the 100-yard dash in 9.8 seconds, fast enough for a school record, but the coach wouldn't give him the record because he said that my brother didn't take first in the race. The coach was the same man who coached football and used us only in blocking practice. Now I felt he really was prejudiced, but there was no way to prove it.

Some Indian boys got picked up for drinking and were put in jail. Dr. Jonas, the president of the college, really looked out for the Indian students at Black Hills State. He knew we were culturally different and had special needs; therefore, he took us under his wing and whenever anybody ever got picked up for drinking, he'd go to the jail and personally counsel them.

At the University of South Dakota, I would just go to the Financial Aid Office and they'd give me all my scholarship money. At Black Hills State, Dr. Jonas took it upon himself to ration our money out. Every Friday, all the Indian students had to line up outside his office. We'd go in one at a time to see him, and he doled out the money to us. We'd come with a long list of items we needed for the weekend. He'd sit there and listen, then he'd check this off and check that off and pretty soon he'd give out $10.00. No matter what a person needed, he would give us only $10.00. He very much rationed the money. Yet, I respected Dr.

Jonas for his insight because a lot of Native American students in a largely non-Native setting need special attention, taking into account their cultural differences. He went out of his way to help. Even in the classes. He saw it as his personal responsibility to counsel us. I did a lot better in school there than I had at USD because the classes were smaller and I received personalized attention. But I know now that my real downfall was my drinking.

THE WARRIOR SOCIETY

I ended up with Dr. Jonas asking me to leave Black Hills State College for fighting while I was intoxicated. He suggested that I go into the military service. In thinking about it, I decided to do it. I packed up all my clothes and left them with my brother, Pānk, then went to the recruiting office and told the recruiter that I wanted to sign up. I ran to the recruiting office because it closed at 5:00 p.m. and I got there at 4:55 p.m. The recruiter gave me a brief test and put me on the bus in Rapid City. The next morning I arrived in Sioux Falls, South Dakota and there I took additional tests and a physical exam. I was twenty-one years old when I went into the service. Most of the boys going in were only eighteen. Being the oldest, I was put in charge of all the recruits.

I vividly remember leaving Sioux Falls for Fort Leonard Wood, Missouri on the bus. On the way down there, it started to snow. As I looked out the window, I became very sad and lonely, thinking to myself, "What in the world did I get myself into?

We got to Fort Leonard Wood, Missouri at about 3:00 a.m. We were led into a reception station. We weren't the only ones arriving on buses: recruits were coming in from all over. Then the army personnel herded us all into what looked like a big airport hangar. They gave us an initiation talk about being in the army and then took us to another building and issued us sheets and blankets. Next, they escorted us over to the barracks and showed us how to make a bed. Well, I knew, from going to a boarding school, how to make a tight bed and bounce a quarter off it. By the time we finished with all of this, it was about 4:30 in the morning. The officer said, "All right, go to bed. You're going to have to get up pretty soon." I knew I'd better get to bed because they were going to be rolling us out any second. I jumped into bed and started snoring right away. Before I went to sleep, though, I saw some of the city boys standing in the bathroom brushing their teeth and putting on their pajamas, just like they were at home.

One boy got all cleaned up to go to bed, and just as he got into bed, the lights came on. The sergeant came in and hollered, "All I want to hear is your feet on the floor. It's time to get up."

The city boy started crying. He said, "I didn't even get to bed yet."

The army tested us for three days to find out what we were qualified to do in the service, and at the end of the three days, only four of us were left in the room. The sergeant came in and said, "All right, you guys are qualified to do whatever you want to do in the service. What to you want to be? Do you want to be an officer, missile man, pilot?"

Well, the first two guys said they wanted to be officers. The third guy said he'd be a pilot.

Then it was my turn. The sergeant said, "Chief, what do you want to do?"

I said, "I want to be a paratrooper." The sergeant about fell over!

He said, "What in the world is wrong with you? Do you have a chip on your shoulder?"

I said, "No sir, I just want to be a paratrooper." To me at that time, it was more honorable to come home and show everybody how strong I was than to flaunt the best education in the world. That's what I wanted to do. I didn't realize it at the time, but I was just acting out the carry-over value of bravery of the traditional Sioux warrior society.

There was a physical training test the army gave at the beginning and at the end of Basic Training. I got the second highest score in it at the end of Basic. The only thing I didn't score high on was grenade throw. It was necessary to lob a grenade right into a bulls-eye. Though I scored low on this part, all the running and jumping things, I maxed.

I remember when we were getting ready to turn our rifles in at the completion of Basic Training, I cleaned mine right away and ran up to see the sergeant. He looked at my rifle and said there was a rust spot on it and told me to clean it again. I went back and as I was cleaning it, I noticed that everybody who went up to see him was getting turned back. So I said to myself, "Heck, I'm just going to wait." I sat back and watched those privates clean their rifle and run up there a second time, only for the sergeant to say, "There's a rust spot right here. Go back and clean it." He was just harassing all the privates.

Later, I went up a second time and he said, "OK, where was it dirty the last time?"

I said, "Right here, Sergeant," and pointed to a spot that was clean.

He looked at it and said, "All right, go on through." I had pulled an old Indian trick on him and had become the first in my unit to finish Basic Training.

After Basic, I went to Ft. Benning, Georgia for Jump School, to be a paratrooper. I traveled by bus and decided to go a day early. I wanted to check out the town to see what it was like. When I got to Columbus, Georgia, which is just outside of Ft. Benning, I walked down the street and began visiting the bars. One particular street had nothing but bars, and above the entrance doors, a sign designated "white only" or "colored only." I went into a "white only" bar and the bartender served me. Then I went into a "colored only" one and couldn't get served. I asked why not and the bartender said it was just for colored people. I said, "Well, I ain't no white man; I'm an American Indian."

He said, "I'm sorry, we can't serve you."

"Let me talk to the owner," I said. The bartender took me into the back room where a big black man was sitting. He was the owner of the place. I explained to him my position. He didn't even talk, just sat there, wearing a three-piece suit, diamond rings on his fingers, a pretty girl standing there rubbing him on the neck. He looked nice. He looked at the bartender and just nodded his head "OK." He didn't say anything. It was like he was a big king. The bartender served me. And I got served in all the bars on that street.

The next morning I got up and caught the bus to Ft. Benning Jump School. I was chewing gum because the night before I had been drinking beer. The sergeant approached me and said, "What do you have in your mouth?"

I quickly swallowed my gum and replied, "Nothing, Sergeant."

He said, "You're chewing gum. You drop and give me ten." I knew he meant ten push-ups. So I got down and did them, then jumped up, kind of with a little smile on my face.

The sergeant said, "Don't you know how to drop? I said drop, Private. Now drop and give me ten."

I knew he wanted me to do another ten push-ups. "OK," I said to myself, so I fell forward, landed on my hands, and did ten push-ups, then got up really proud.

Again, he said, "Private, don't you know how to drop?"

A trooper was walking by and the sergeant said, "Trooper, show this private how to drop." That trooper jumped out in mid-air. He landed on his toes and fingertips, knocked out ten push-ups, jumped up, saluted and went on.

The sergeant looked at me and said, "OK, Private, I want to see you drop." So I jumped up in the air and landed right on my face. I got a mouth full of dirt, but I knocked out ten push-ups before I got up.

Now the sergeant said, "I didn't hear one for airborne. Drop and give me ten more." I jumped in mid-air and almost landed on my face again. I did ten more push-ups, then got up. I had done forty push-ups in the first few moments of arriving at Jump School!

I remember the first morning we had reveille and inspection. A jump cadre had come around behind me and poked me in the back of the head, saying, "You've got a long hair! You have a long hair and you have a thread hanging off your buttons!" He continued, "You'll get a gig for this. Now drop and give me ten push-ups." That night I shaved my head and used a cigarette lighter to burn all those loose threads.

There was a marine next to me in the ranks in Jump School. He was very cocky and thought he was tougher than any of the other paratroopers. One day a jump cadre said to him, "Drop and give me ten."

He looked at the jump cadre and said, "Which arm, Sergeant?"

That did it! The sergeant said, "I'll tell you what, Private. You get down there and do push-ups until I get tired."

In Jump School, everybody is assigned a number. One has no name, just a number. The powers-that-be took this cocky marine's helmet number and passed it to all the other jump cadre so they could harass the guy all day long. A week later, the tough marine washed out.

We had a speed march at the end of Jump School. Our trainers called it a march, but it was really a run. It was 102° and humid. We were told to take salt tablets because of the heat. We began the speed march and must have run about three miles. As I said previously, I can't run very far. Anyway, when we were getting close to the finish, all of a sudden, I started seeing spots. The guys on each side of me were saying, "Come on, Chief; come on, Chief, you can make it." With their encouragement, I just kept on going. I became very dizzy and, pretty soon, I fell down.

When I looked up, the platoon was still running, so I started to get up to rejoin the men. The second platoon was coming from behind, and the sergeant from that platoon came running up and grabbed me, then threw me in the ditch. He said, "Get out of the way, leg." (If a trooper can't make it through Jump School, he is known as a leg.)

I came crawling out of that ditch and ran to catch up with my platoon. They had just arrived at the finish line and were standing at attention. The trainers were calling off their helmet numbers to see who had finished. I got in the ranks just when they called my number and was, thus, able to qualify for the final week, known as Jump Week, because that is when troopers do the actual parachute jumps.

The first time I jumped out of an airplane was also the first time I had ever flown in one. It was an old flying boxcar, a C-119. We got in it, the pilot started it up, and that old thing began rattling. The walls were shaking; everything, in fact, was rattling. We took off down the runway, using up every bit of it and then some. We barely went over the fence at the other end of the runway as we got up in the air. I told the jump sergeant that I'd like to be the first jumper out the door. He said, "OK, Chief, come up here."

Well, a young second lieutenant there was there, and he must have just finished Officer Candidate School. His eyes were big and round, and he apparently couldn't be outdone. He said, "I want to be first." So the sergeant had to let him jump first.

I remember looking around the aircraft and noticing that everybody had big eyes. I just thought to myself, "Maybe I've got big eyes too." My first jump was exciting. I was happy and proud because now I could be considered a warrior among my people.

After Jump School, before I went to my regular assignment, I came home on leave to show off my paratrooper wings and jump boots. (Only those who have graduated from Jump School can wear paratrooper wings and jump boots.) When my leave was over, my Uncle Kenny said, "Well, where are they sending you for assignment?"

U.S. Paratrooper Insignia

I automatically replied, "Germany." I didn't really know where I was going, not having received my orders yet.

But when I got back to my unit and got my assignment, it was Germany. It was like I knew where I was going to go before I received my official orders.

When I left for Germany, I got on a military air transport and flew from New Jersey. We landed in the Azores for refueling, then went on and landed in Paris the next morning. I'll never forget flying in over Paris. The pilot flew us around the Eiffel Tower and when I looked down, it seemed like every roof had red tile. We refueled there and then went on to Frankfurt.

In Frankfurt, our leaders took us to the transit billets where we had orientation about how to conduct ourselves in Germany. They had given us a little booklet when we were on the plane. It contained German phrases that we could learn, just basic German sentences.

They gave us a couple hours off the first afternoon so we could go touring in Frankfurt. We received two-hour passes. A few of us went to the first Gasthaus we saw. We were sitting there and everybody ordered a beer. We gave our waitress a dollar and she returned some funny-looking coins to us. We didn't know if we had received the correct change or not. A couple of German girls were sitting at the next table. The guys I was with got out their little German book and read the German phrases, trying to ask the girls to come join us for a drink. Finally, when the girls did not respond, one of the guys said, "Heck, just ask them in English."

The other guy said, "Would you ladies care to join us for a drink?"

The girls said, "No thank you."

The guy threw his book down. He said, "That's it. I made a fool out of myself trying to speak German. I'll never try that again." Actually, in Germany at that time (1962), very little English was spoken.

We left Frankfurt by train to go to Mainz-Gonsenheim. That's where I was to be stationed. The train we rode on was an old steam engine. As we traveled on the train, I looked out the window because I wanted to see everything. There was a sign above the window in German. I didn't know what it said, but I had stuck my head out the window when I suddenly got a cinder in my eye. I had a heck of a time getting that cinder out! Cinders were blowing back from the steam engine smokestack. What the sign above the window said was, "Beware of cinders. Don't lean out the window."

In Mainz-Gonsenheim, I was stationed at Lee Barracks, the home of the Airborne in Europe. I was assigned to Headquarters Company, 505 Paratrooper Brigade, which was attached to the 8th Division in Europe. It just so happened that Headquarters Company was the best parade unit in Europe at that time. The company commander would have us practice passing in review every day. We were the best marchers in Europe. Every weekend the commander got us up at 4:00 a.m. on Saturday and trucked us someplace in Germany for a parade. We'd get out, march, pass and review. We had to spit-shine our boots and dress up every weekend. We did that for almost a year, but finally in 1963 the Army switched us over to Airborne Mechanized.

Then we became the 509th and finally received military training.

When I first got to Germany, five Deutsche Marks equaled $1.00. That meant that a dollar went a long way in Germany at that time. I recall I could get a bottle of beer for one mark, a really cheap price. Shopping in the German stores, I noticed that the prices were written in marks, of course, and they were indicated in thousands of marks. I just couldn't get over it! I didn't know how much the prices were in dollars, but I'll always remember the huge-looking prices in Deutsche Marks.

I have a clear memory of going on a weekend pass to Frankfurt one time. I got off the train, came out of the station, turned to the left, and started walking down the street. I hadn't gone too far when I saw three Germans beating up another German. This was when I first arrived in Germany and couldn't afford any civilian clothes, so I was wearing my uniform. When I saw the fight, I ran over there and said, "All right, you bastards, you want to gang up on somebody? Gang up on me!" I took off my army blouse and tore into those three guys. The German who was getting beat up joined me in running the other three down the street. A spectator standing nearby saw my army blouse lying on the ground, picked it up, and brushed it off. He thought it was very disrespectful for me to leave my army blouse on the ground. The other fellow, though, was so thankful for me helping him out that he invited me to his home for supper. He could speak a little English; his wife and her sister could not. Come to find out, he was a Jew, and these other three Germans were beating him up because he was a Jew. While at his home for supper, he kept talking to his sister-in-law to encourage her to be nice to me, but we had a language barrier. I thanked him for the meal and left.

While in the military, drinking alcohol became a regular habit for me. I believe, in fact, that that's when I really became a hard-core alcoholic. I started drinking routinely when I was in high school and I really didn't think about being an alcoholic. But once I got to Germany, I drank even more.

I'd always end up having to borrow money every month when I was in the service because I spent all of mine on booze. One of the guys I would borrow money from was what would be termed a "loan shark." (One borrows money from a loan shark for 100% interest; if a person borrows $10, then he pays back $20.) I went to this loan shark by the name of Moose Nelson. Moose was from Minnesota and was a great big lumberjack-looking guy. He said, "Chief, you borrow money from me every month. Here, I'll tell you what I'll do. I'll help you get started in the loan shark business."

I think he lent me $100 to get started in the business. People would come and borrow money from me and I'd say, "OK, here's $20, and now you owe me $40." On payday, I was supposed to collect my money. Well, we were standing at the end of the line where the guys got paid. They'd come out and Moose would collect his money. Then I'd make an attempt to collect my money, but everybody who owed me would come up with these sad stories. Finally, I said, "Just give me the money I lent you." I eventually made my money back and repaid Moose. I guess I just had too soft a heart to succeed as a loan shark.

People in the service called me "Chief." I didn't mind that because I knew they didn't know anything about American Indians. All they knew is what they saw in Hollywood movies. All Indians in the army are probably called Chief. Back home in the border towns around the reservation, when locals call a person Chief, anyone can tell by the tone of their voice that the name carries a negative connotation. It's usually clear what is meant. While I was in the service, though, I didn't mind being called Chief because it wasn't negative. It was just that my army buddies thought they were doing me a favor by calling me Chief.

One of the guys I ran around in the Army with was named Smitty. He was a regular hillbilly from West Virginia. He was a big guy and crazier than heck. He had two pairs of boxing gloves. When he came back from drinking in town, he'd bring out those gloves. Then he'd go around the company and throw them at someone and say, "OK, put these on, you and me is going to fight."

Well, normally on the weekend I'd be out somewhere, but it so happened one Saturday night I had stayed home--I don't know why--and here came Smitty, feeling his oats. He threw his gloves at me and said, "Put these on, Chief; you and me's going to fight."

I hearkened back to my dad's advice, "If you're forced into a fight, don't run from it." Therefore, I decided to accept Smitty's challenge.

The man who slept above me in the bunkbed was also a hillbilly by the name of Owens. Owens hated Smitty because Smitty used to call him (Owens) a dumb hillbilly. Smitty was a hillbilly himself; he was just teasing Owens. Anyway, Owens couldn't take it and he hated Smitty's guts. Owens was helping put on my gloves and laced them up. He said, "You can get him, Chief; you can get him." He continued, "Just jab him and stay away from him." So that's what I did. When we started fighting, I just jabbed him. He was a big guy and I knew darn well if I tried to go toe-to-toe with him, he'd knock me out. Thus, I'd just jab and get away, jab and get away. Surprisingly, I got in a lucky punch and hit Smitty right on the tip of his nose. It gave him a nosebleed. Members of the company had started gathering around when we were fighting, and it looked like I was winning because Smitty had a bloody nose and blood was all over him. I realized that he was getting mad when he started charging me. He got me in the corner once and caught me alongside the head.

I saw stars and thought to myself that I had to get out of that corner: I ducked down and pushed my way out. I said to myself, "If someone were to look at this fight, it seems like I'm winning. I know what I'm going to do; I'm going to pull an old Indian trick."

I told Smitty, "I quit; I quit, Smitty. You win. I give up. You win." I stopped right there and the way it appeared, it seemed I had won, but in actuality, if we had gone any further, I think I would have lost.

After that, Smitty became my best buddy. He would come and get me in the evenings or on weekends and say, "Come on, Chief, let's go to town." Away we'd go. Smitty, one of my best buddies, was Ralph Smitson, from West ("by God," as he always said) Virginia.

My friend, Smitty, and I, one weekend, had gone downtown bar hopping and went into a bar called the Hillbilly Club in downtown Mainz-Gonsenheim. All at once, he said, "Chief, watch my back. There's some guys over here trying to horn in on our girls."

I asked, "What do you mean, our girls?"

He replied, "Well, this is our joint and those are our girls, and those legs are trying to horn in on our girls." He went over and started a ruckus. Before I knew it, the whole place was in a free-for-all. Naturally, I joined in to help my buddy. We were going toe-to-toe with some legs and it suddenly dawned on me that the MPs were coming.

I hollered at Smitty, "Let's get out of here; the MPs are coming." I didn't know if they were or not; it just came to me that they were on their way.

We started running out the front door and, just then, the MPs pulled up in their jeeps and jumped out. I was thinking to myself, "I've got to act fast here."

I quickly ran out into the street and shouted at them, "Hey, you MPs!" I pointed, "Over here, this is where they're fighting." Boy, they came running right past us and into the Hillbilly Club. As soon as they went by us, we took off

69

down the street. The MPs reminded me of the Keystone Cops.

I remember we were going on a NATO exercise in Turkey. We had flown to Adana, Turkey, which is close to the Syrian border. We marshalled there for two weeks with the Greek and Turkish paratroopers. During that time the Greeks and Turks were giving demonstrations on their combat effectiveness. When I saw how combat-ready they were and realized how soft the U.S. Army was, I just thought, "Oh no, if we ever go to war, I don't want to go because we'll lose." But the company commander of "A Company" thought he had the fastest company in Europe. He prided himself on his company's running ability and wasn't afraid to challenge anyone in Europe. I was told he had played football at West point. Well, he challenged the Turks and Greeks to a twelve-mile speed march. All three companies lined up. The official fired a gun and off everyone went. The Turks and Greeks ran circles around "A Company."

We stayed there in Adana for two weeks, then flew up across the isthmus to the northern part of Turkey. We jumped in with the Greek and Turkish paratroopers right near the Greek/Turkish border. From there, we walked for another week to a little town called Uzunköprü. Just before we got to Uzunköprü, we met up with the Turkish Army. It was just like a Hollywood movie. One evening we were walking along this little valley, we looked up a hill on the horizon, and there stood a long string of horses. The Turkish Army was on horseback. They came riding down and wanted cigarettes: cigarettes for this, cigarettes for that. We had small packs of C-ration cigarettes, four cigarettes in a pack. I offered one of the Turks a pack in exchange for riding his horse. He let me do it. I rode his horse up and down the road. Some of the guys in my platoon had their eyes bugging out, questioning, "Chief, you know how to ride a horse?"

I answered, "Yes, we have a lot of horses back home on the reservation. Everybody grows up riding horses."

The Turks' rifles, their saddles and bridles were U.S. Army issue. I realized that this was all old army equipment that the U.S. government had given to Turkey. Their rifles were old bolt-action Springfields. I also recognized the saddles. We used to have that kind of saddle out on the reservation, around the old Bureau of Indian Affairs horse barn.

When we got to Uzunköprü, we boarded the train for Istanbul. The bathroom on the train was a little room with just a hole in the floor and a footprint on each side. Everything fell down on the tracks.

We pulled into Istanbul and it seemed like everybody in town was waiting for us. They had everything imaginable for sale. They didn't want money, only cigarettes. The U.S. Army officials had told us, "Don't eat the food, don't drink the water, don't drink the wine or you'll get sick." Well, a lot of guys did get the runs from eating what they weren't supposed to eat.

Our first night in Istanbul, several of the guys were going over the wall. They were sneaking off to check out the town. There were no passes allowed, and they were going

71

AWOL. I was getting ready to leave when the sergeant noticed. He said, "Chief, if you stay, I'll put you next in line for a sergeant stripe." I decided not to go over the wall. I missed out going to town, but those who went AWOL got an Article 15 (formal charge) when they returned.

That winter I went on leave to Amsterdam, Holland. When I got off the train, I didn't realize it at first, but it seemed like everybody had a bicycle. It looked like there were 1,000 bicycles in front of the train station. There were very few cars. Later, I saw that the streets were very narrow, and I guess that's why so many people rode bikes. I took a boat tour up and down the canals of Amsterdam. I enjoyed Holland because the people spoke English and it wasn't difficult to get around.

One afternoon, I was bar hopping in Amsterdam. I went into a bar and saw some American Indians sitting at the table. I was excited, went over and introduced myself, and joined them. They were Cree Indians from Canada and were stationed in the Canadian Air Force in Holland. After a few drinks, one of them said to me, "You are our enemy."

I asked, "Me?"

He replied, "Yes, the Sioux are our enemy."

I thought to myself, "How can I be his enemy? I've never even heard of the Cree." I left, though, before he got belligerent.

One boy in my platoon always teased me about being Mongolian. He said, "You're a Chinese because you guys came across the Bering Straights."

I countered, "No, we did not come across the Bering Straights; we've always been in North America." Next, he began calling me Chinaman Joe. One morning at reveille, I got tired of him calling me by that name, and I challenged him on it. We ended up in a fight there in the ranks. It was just a brief fight, but after that, he never called me Chinaman Joe any more. I guess I got his respect. I explained to him that we have our own history about where we came from, and it's not our belief we crossed the Bering Straits.

TREATED LIKE KINGS

One summer while I was in the army, I had taken leave and gone to Paris. Chris Paquette, one of my buddies, and I jumped on a train and left for Paris. From there, we went to St. Mère Eglíse. We had always heard about this place. It was the first town liberated in France during World War II, having been liberated by Headquarters Company, 505 Paratroopers, which was the unit we were in at the time. I had talked Chris into going to visit St. Mère Église, which is located on the coast of Normandy.

The train only went as far as a town called Chef Dupont (Chef means headman in French; the word *chief* comes from *chef*), about ten kilometers from St. Mère Église. We got off there. A county fair was going on when we arrived. We tried to get a hotel room, but everything was filled up, and the hotel owner let us sleep in his room. I don't know where he slept.

At the county fair, there was a carnival. I remember that a group of kids was following us around, no doubt attracted by our uniforms The carnival had a shooting gallery. I paid and got up there to shoot. Every time I shot, one of the targets went down. I ended up with a perfect score and won a prize, which I gave to a little boy who was standing beside me. His eyes were so big with wonderment, he must have thought I was the best shot in the world.

We got hungry and went into a little restaurant. We couldn't read French, couldn't speak French, and didn't have any idea what to order. We looked around and made it known what we wanted by pointing at the food other people were eating. That's what the waiter brought us, and that's how we got our meals.

Finally a guy who could speak a little English came walking in the door. He was the sheriff, and we visited with him a little bit. We told him we wanted to go to St. Mère Église. He said the only way was by taxi.

When we got to St. Mère Église, we were treated like kings. The people running the hotel bought us free beer when we got there. At the restaurant, we were given a free meal. Everyplace we went, the people smiled and bragged about us. After visiting in that little town, we decided to walk down to the Utah Beachhead. It was a pretty good walk. It must have been six or seven kilometers to the beach. At the beachhead, there were a lot of rusted armored personnel carriers that had been destroyed and left there during World War II.

Paratrooper Kings

There was a museum in the town of St. Mère Église itself, with the roof built in a parachute shape. Information gave the history of the area during the invasion. The paratroopers jumped in early in the morning on June 7, 1944. The whole area around the town had been flooded, and many paratroopers drowned. Five thousand paratroopers, in all, had died that night in June 1944. Even so, the town was still able to be liberated. It was really a miracle that occurred there, and the local French people will always remember what was done for them.

In 1964, the Winter Olympics games were held in Innsbruck, Austria. Chris and I took leave to go there. When we got to Innsbruck, every hotel in town was full, forcing us to get back on the train and return over the mountains to Germany. At the first little town in Germany, we bailed out and found a Gasthaus that had some rooms. We'd stay there at night and then get on the first train in the morning to go back over the mountains to Innsbruck. We were spectators at the Winter Olympics during the day. Then we'd catch the last train to Germany and ride back to the small German town. I couldn't get over the fact that every little Gasthaus was very crowded. People seemed to be partying everywhere.

On another occasion, I went to Garmisch-Partenkirchen Garden. The U.S. Army had a ski resort there, on the Zugspitze, the highest mountain in Germany. I went up the mountain by ski lift, then I'd fall all the way down. Finally, I decided I'd better take some ski lessons. I did, and on the second day, I went up and began skiing down halfway decently. I remember I was coming down pretty well when right at the end of the slope there was a drop-off about three feet high. A group of girls was lined up, waiting for the ski lift. As I came off that three-foot drop, I went up in the air and landed like a hunk of ice, knocking the wind out of me. I was hurt, but I couldn't let all those girls know that the paratrooper was hurt. I got up, forced a smile, and brushed off the snow. That evening I soaked in the bathtub and went straight to bed. I did enjoy learning how to ski, though.

There are a lot of woods in Germany, and the people really take pride in their forests. Once, on maneuvers in the woods on a Sunday, we were given time off to do whatever we wanted. I said to my buddy, Chris, "Let's go for a walk."

78

As we left, I noticed a deer hunting stand by a large and tall pine tree. I remarked, "OK, this is where we're leaving from. Remember this spot."

I took Chris in a big circle for about three hours, after which he said, "Chief, we'd better turn back now; we'd better go back."

I commented, "Well, we're almost back."

He said, "No, no, we'd better turn around and go back now."

Finally, we got to the same tree we had left from and I said, "OK, we're back where we started from."

Chris said, "Nah, come on, Chief, don't play games."

I replied, "I'm not. Remember that deer hunting stand when we left for our walk? It's right on the other side of that tree."

He said again, "Now come on, Chief don't play games."

I said, "OK then, I'll bet you a case of beer." We made the bet and I said, "Now go to the other side of that tree."

When he went around to the other side and saw the deer hunting stand, his mouth fell open and he asked, "How did you do that?"

I said, "Heck, I got time and grade in the woods. I go deer hunting all the time at home."

He never got over that. City boys are like that; they seem to get lost easily. Growing up on the reservation, one gains a lot of experience in the woods, learning to develop one's instincts to help in finding one's way around there.

In Germany, the beer was always served at room temperature. If a person wanted a cold beer, the only place it could be had was at a GI bar.

Whenever we came off the post on payday, it seemed like a hundred peddlers stood there trying to sell us something: suits, cars, pens, watches, cuckoo clocks, prostitutes, you name it. On payday, the prices would double. The day before payday, a person could buy something for $2.00. Then, the very next day, the same item cost $4.00. That lasted for two or three days and then by the end of the month, prices went way down again.

While I was living in Germany, I noticed that above the doors of the homes, people marked the year it was built, many of them showing dates of 1730 and 1740. I even saw a building that had been constructed in the 1600's. I wondered how in the world a building could last so long. One year, someone started to build a house right across the street from the barracks. At first, they built a foundation and then let it sit for about six months. I wondered what was going on. Then they came back and put up the big wooden frame and let it sit for another six months. They put a small evergreen tree up on top, with colored flags tied to it, and I really wondered what was going on. (The evergreen with its flags, I learned, was some sort of religious symbol, kind of like keeping the evil spirits away.) Finally, they came back about six months later to finish building the house. It took them almost two years to build that house! I started asking around and found out later that it used to take three or four years to build a house. Each part would take a year: the foundation, the frame, and the completion of the building. That's one of the reasons the houses are so old. People took their time building them.

Right outside Lee Barracks was a little Gasthaus that we used to go to, called Luna Gardens. A small clique of us hung out there and drank beer almost every evening. In those days, all the beer bottles had pop tops, little ceramic lids that fit in the bottle opening and were held down by a wire frame attached to the bottle. The Germans didn't have beer cans then. Well, I discovered that if I opened these pop tops very quickly, the ceramic lid could swing around and break the top of the bottle right off. I used to bet somebody that with one finger, I could strike the ceramic lid and break the neck off. Their answer would be, "No way!"

I'd say, "I'll bet you a case of beer." Then I'd use my knuckle, making like I was hitting the lid to pop it open. My knuckle would actually hit the wire frame; then the ceramic lid would spring around and break the top off the bottles. I won a lot of free beers with that trick. I never told the guys how I did it, making them believe I was a tough paratrooper.

Another way I used to get free beer was to hop over tables. During my high school days, I had set several records in the high jump; thus, to jump over a table was easy for me. I'd point and say, "I can stand right here and hop over this table." No one believed me, so I'd bet them a case of beer, stand before the table, then leap over it without my feet touching the top surface at all.

Still another method of getting free beer was that we dared each other to steal MP vehicles, though we didn't actually steal them. When the MP would pull up to check out the Gasthaus, we'd just jump in and drive the vehicle around the corner, hiding it from them. I hid the first one; then another one of the guys in our clique had to take his turn. When my turn came again, I chose a ¾-ton truck to hide from the MPs. I jumped in and started driving down the road. When I tried to turn, the truck wouldn't turn because the wheel had been chained. The MPs got wise to us and started chaining the wheels. Instead of turning, then, I just drove straight ahead for about six blocks and parked the truck. After that, I gave up hiding MP vehicles.

We did crazy things just to break the monotony and to win a couple of free beers. My buddy, Smitty, was a mechanic when on duty. We got a couple of old junk cars, pieced together one car, and got it running. It was an old Opel convertible. Since only sergeants and above were allowed to have vehicles, we used to sneak-drive around the post; but one day, we decided to drive the car off-post. Before we could, though, it had to have license plates and a sticker. We stole a license plate from the front of one car and one with a number that was almost the same from the back of another car. I got some pens, colors, and sticker material, made a sticker that looked just like a regular military sticker, and put it on the windshield. We decided to draw straws to see who of the four of us--Smitty, Chris, Doug Werner and myself--was going to drive the Opel off-post. Next, we all rehearsed what we were going to say when we pulled up at the main gate. If the MP started questioning us, we had to have our story straight. Well, we all four got in our car, with Smitty and me in the front seat. We pulled up at the front gate and got ready for the questioning, but, lo and behold, the MP waved us right through. We drove out, turned down the street, and when we got out of sight, we all hollered for joy. All weekend we drove our little car around town and really had a ball. The first thing we wanted to do was to give the fräuleins a ride. After the weekend, though, we decided on Monday that we had better hide the car before we got caught. At least, we had one weekend of cruising with the fräuleins.

In the basement of our barracks was a snack bar, run by the company, that also served beer. I had a beer tab; thus, if I ran out of money, I could charge beer there. Well, it reached a point where a lot of people were charging beer, but nobody was paying their tab. As a result, the first sergeant cut everybody off. No more free beer.

Well, one night I came back to the barracks halfway drunk and out of money, ran down to the company snack bar, and ordered up. I said, "Put it on my tab."

The clerk said, "No more free beer."

I questioned, "Who said that?"

"First Sergeant," I was told.

I went upstairs to the duty sergeant and asked, "Do you have the first sergeant's phone number?"

He replied, "Yeah, why?"

"Because I want to talk to him," I said.

"No, no," he pleaded, "don't do that."

I insisted, "Give me the first sergeant's number. I want to talk to him."

Finally, he got the number and put in the call. I picked up the phone and said, "First Sergeant, this is Chief Ross. I'd like to know why we've been cut off on beer tabs. I pay my tab every month." I really gave him a story.

He said, "OK, give me the duty sergeant."

I gave the phone back to him and, as the first sergeant talked to him, the duty sergeant began turning red-faced. "Yes, Sergeant. Yes, Sergeant," he was saying.

He hung up and said to me, "Come on."

"Well what did he say?" I wanted to know.

He replied, "He told me to give that damn Indian enough beer until it comes out his f'en ears." I was the only one in the company who got to charge up more beer. The first sergeant liked me. Because a Lakota boy from South Dakota had saved his life during World War II, he kind of favored me. But I used his favoritism in the wrong way: to be the only one able to charge beer at the snack bar.

SILENT NIGHT, HOLY NIGHT

Christmas in Germany was really something! I liked it because it was celebrated as a religious holiday. No stores were open; in fact, nothing was open in town except for the churches. Christmas decorations were all white. None of the multicolored decorations like we have, just pure-white.

Chris Paquette wanted a Christmas tree but didn't have enough money to buy one. He and I decided, therefore, that we were going to "borrow" one from a German Christmas tree lot off-post. We sneaked out one night, he jumped on my shoulders, and reached over the fence to get a Christmas tree. It seemed like he was taking forever. I said, "Hurry up! What's taking you so long?" I looked up and here he was, picking up Christmas trees and looking at them one by one. I said, "Hey, when you're stealing a tree, you don't get picky; you just grab one and go."

We finally chose a tree and took it back to the barracks. We decorated it like kids do in grade school, with chains made out of colored paper. That was our platoon Christmas tree. We had made a stand by just nailing boards to the bottom of the tree so that when we put it up, it dried out very quickly. In the evenings when the boys came back from off-post, they'd stagger into our tree and knock the pine needles off. Very soon, our Christmas tree became an *unšika* (pitiful) skeleton. Almost all the needles were knocked off.

I remember on Christmas Eve we all gathered around this skeleton tree, all feeling sad. Chris said, "Let's sing some Christmas songs." We sang "Silent Night, Holy Night..." and then we stopped.

Chris asked, "What's wrong? How come you guys aren't singing the rest of it?"

We said, "That's all we know."

"Well let's sing 'O Little Town of Bethlehem,'" Chris suggested. We all sang "O Little Town of Bethlehem..." and everybody stopped again.

"Now what's wrong?"

We said, "Well, that's all we know." We ended up singing about four or five Christmas carol titles and called it a night.

Unšika Christmas Tree

I got a Christmas package from my mother. She must've thought I was in the front lines of a war or something because she sent socks, hankies, soap, toothpaste. She also put some cookies in the package. I was the only one in my platoon who got a Christmas package. Well, the guys all gathered around when I was opening it. Chris jumped on top of me and then everybody grabbed my present and ripped it open. We all ate the cookies, enjoying every bite. I guess all the guys wished they had a Christmas present too.

Another holiday in Mainz, Germany is a pre-Lenten celebration called Fasching. It really has a carnival atmosphere where everybody dresses up and parties. It's noted throughout Germany as a very good party time. Then nine months later, a lot of babies are born.

I remember one time I went on leave to Holland with a Hawaiian buddy of mine named Army Gill. We had gone to the North Sea because he wanted to go surfing, but when we got there, the waves were only about six feet high. He complained about the waves the whole time we were there.

One night when we were sitting in a bar hustling chicks, Army Gill told them he was a Hawaiian. Boy, the chicks really liked that! So I told them I was a Sioux Indian. As soon as I said that, they all became afraid of me. They would go, "Wooo wooo," with their hands over their mouths. Maybe they thought I was going to scalp them. I learned my lesson. When we went out the next night, I told the girls I was a Hawaiian too, the only difference being that my father owned a pineapple ranch. Well, as soon as I mentioned that, I had chicks hanging all over me. I guess they thought they were going to get to go to Hawaii to a pineapple ranch.

Germany is famous for its cuckoo clocks. I remember going to a store in Wiesbaden where the entire store was a giant cuckoo clock. The door where you entered the store was where the little bird would pop out. When I walked in, I noticed there must have been 1,000 cuckoo clocks hanging up in that little store. I started to collect them, buying one every payday. They were only about $10.00, so I bought about a dozen of them. I don't know what my fascination was with the cuckoo clock. Maybe it was an interest in the unusual.

One morning when we were out on maneuvers, I heard a cuckoo bird out in the woods. I jumped out of the sack to go look for it. The rest of the guys in my platoon questioned, "Where the hell are you going?"

I said, "I'm going to find that cuckoo bird." They said there was no such thing, that it was just a little bird on a clock.

"No," I insisted, "I heard it. It's the real thing." I went out in the woods to search for it and finally found it. It looked like a long-necked screech owl and was grayish in color.

When we got back from Turkey, my platoon sergeant made me a squad leader because, as he said, I was next in line for E-5 sergeant stripes. We went on maneuvers, Red Army versus Blue Army. I was head of a ground surveillance radar team. Our rookie lieutenant said, "Ross, I want you to set your radar right here and look down this road. Tell me when the enemy is approaching."

I said, "Sir, we could hear somebody coming down this road before this radar would pick it up."

He got angry with me and said, "You set up right here and don't you question me."

"Sir, we'll set up here, but we're just sitting ducks waiting to be captured," I answered. Well, he really got angry then! So we followed our orders and set up operations as instructed. Since it was ground surveillance radar, it was only able to pick up things in the line of sight. If the enemy came sneaking up behind the trees or behind the hill, the radar wouldn't pick them up. Sure enough, that's what happened. Before we could even move, we got captured. Our captors hauled us back and put us in the big open area with concertina wire all around us and made us take off our boots so we wouldn't run away. Next, they wanted us to give up our boots.

We said, "Hell no, we aren't giving up our boots."

"Well, we'll come in there and get them," they countered.

We challenged, "Come in here and try to take them then." They never did. I guess those "legs" were afraid of us.

The next day they put us on KP. All during these war games, we were nice and warm in the mess tent, eating hot food. Everybody else was freezing in foxholes, so maybe it paid off for us to get captured since it was only a game.

In another incident, I was a jeep driver for the first sergeant. Like I said before, I was kind of a pet to him; thus, he said to me, "Come on, Chief, let's go." I drove him around to all the different outposts. When we came back to headquarters, he said, "OK, get yourself a little sleep, and then we'll head out again." I put my head on the steering wheel and tried to sleep. While I was dozing off, it started to rain. I put on my poncho, but then it started to rain hard, so I got down under the jeep to sleep. It turned out there was a little indentation in the ground under the jeep that began to fill up with water. The next thing I knew, I was soaking wet. I crawled out of there, all angry and wet, and I went over to the mess tent to get me a cup of hot coffee. I went to drink it and burned my lip, the coffee having made the metal

90

canteen cup hot. I was doubly angry now and was really cursing the army by then!

I got halfway dried off by the time the first sergeant came back and said, "Let's go." I went out to the jeep and discovered I had a flat tire. I had to change it in the rain. I was cold, wet and had a burned lip. I was triple-angry at the army by then!

Once we were pulling border duty at the east/west German border near Freiburg. We spent three days out on the border and came in for three days. We did that for about a month at a time once a year. We had just pulled three days and had come off the border and cleaned up our gear. We all headed for the EM (Enlisted Men) Club. We were sitting there drinking beer, when all of a sudden, the NCO in charge came out on the stage and said, "OK, this is an alert. Everybody report to your unit." Well, nobody budged. Everybody just kept drinking beer and having a good time. He spoke again, but this time he said, "All right, this is an alert. Everybody will report to your unit right now. No more beers will be sold." Well, this time some of the guys started getting up and heading out, but grumbling. Most of the guys just stayed there and didn't move.

The third time the NCO made the announcement, he said, "The president of the United States has been shot. You will report to your unit immediately." The whole place stood up. Everybody started running into each other, dashing every direction, trying to get out of there. I made it back to my bay and got my team together, but I had too much beer under my belt. One of the platoon sergeants had to take over for me and drive us to the border that night.

We were still on the border when Thanksgiving came. The army said they were going to bring us hot turkey dinner, with mashed potatoes and gravy that they'd fly in by helicopter. Well, our outpost was at the end of the line. By the time they got that hot Thanksgiving dinner to us, it was cold: everything was cold. I just took some cold turkey and made a sandwich. Everybody was grumbling, not wanting cold potatoes and gravy. We went back to our foxhole. We had C-rations with a little heater unit, so we set the heater on fire and warmed up a can of beans. We ate beans with cold turkey sandwiches for Thanksgiving that year.

One day, a German came up to the company commander and invited all the Indian boys in the company to come to a meeting. The commander told all of us to get dressed in our Class "A" uniforms to attend the meeting. Well, come to find out, these Germans were Indian hobbyists who studied American Indians. They asked me where I was from, and I told them I was from Pine Ridge, South Dakota. When they found out I was a Sioux Indian, they said, "We're studying about your people." I guess they studied different tribes and this one group was studying the Sioux.

One person said, "I want you to come to our meeting and talk to us about the history and culture of your people. In particular, I'm interested in the Battle of Slim Buttes." Well, I didn't remember any Battle of Slim Buttes, but I knew where Slim Buttes was, since I went deer hunting there.

As far as telling about the history and culture of my people, that's when I realized that I couldn't do it because I had grown up a Christian and studied only U.S. Government and U.S. History. I hadn't really had an opportunity to study my own history. The incident was a great awakening for me. It planted a seed in me to start studying my own history. That's when I started a search for my roots.

On New Year's Eve in 1963, I was in Wiesbaden, Germany. A wooden Indian marked the entrance of the dance floor at a certain Gasthaus. I told my buddy I was going to steal the statue. He said, "You could never get by with it."

"Wait and see," I replied. At midnight on New Year's Eve when everybody started hollering, hugging, kissing, and celebrating, I grabbed that wooden Indian, and up the stairs I went. I got it outside and called a taxicab over. At first, the driver didn't want to take it, but when I offered him extra dollars, he loaded me up and took me back to the post. Not being able to take the statue through the front gate, I threw it over the fence, went around to get it, then hauled it back to my room.

Later I dressed it up like a first sergeant paratrooper. I put stripes on it and a name tag with the name "Kaw-liga." ("Kaw-liga, the Wooden Indian" is the name of a country/western song.) A Sioux friend of mine from Fort Peck, Montana came with his buddies and stole Kaw-liga one weekend. Then I got my buddies and we went to "A" Company and stole him back. We began a fight over that wooden Indian. He soon became a platoon mascot. We put him in our bay where we kept all our equipment so that no one could steal him when we weren't around.

Wooden Indian

In 1964, some recruiters came around looking for helicopter pilots. They had checked everybody's records, and they said to me, "We see here that you're qualified to go to helicopter school. Would you like to go?"

I said, "Let me think about it." They took a small group of us in and gave us a pep talk. Five of us decided to go to chopper school. We were sitting outside a major's office, waiting to go in, one by one, to sign up. Fort Rucker, Alabama was the site for those who signed up for training. I was the last one waiting to see the major, and a voice inside my head kept saying to me, "Don't do it, Chuck." When it was my turn to go in and sign the papers, I decided not to, I just got up and went back to the barracks. The following year, Vietnam officially opened up and chopper pilots were number-one targets for the Viet Cong. I believe the spirits (guardian angels) told me not to sign up for chopper school.

My Sioux buddy, Tom Duran, from "A" Company used to come over to see me after he'd been out drinking. He would awaken me at 3:00 or 4:00 in the morning. He'd have a bottle of wine and would want to drink. I didn't have to drink with him; but, out of politeness, I would sit up with him and have a few drinks. The next thing we'd do was to roust everybody out in the platoon, and we'd start singing Indian and dancing Indian. Pretty soon, we'd make all the white boys dance. I remember one white boy, Doug Werner, threw his hands in the air and started hopping up and down, chanting, "Rain, rain, rain."

We sometimes had mini-pow-wows at the bars that Duran, José Rael from New Mexico and I would put on. I'd be the announcer. Other times, I would announce like we were having a rodeo. We'd go through the whole procedure of running the bulls into the chutes. We positioned the chairs into a make-believe chute, and we'd sit down on the center chair like we were sitting down on a bull. We'd open the gate and start bucking the chairs. I don't know how many chairs we broke by doing that. The owner of Luna Gardens, Mr. Roman Martin, used to really get angry with us. He'd run us out of there, exclaiming, "You GIs are crazy in the head!"

In 1964, a number of race riots occurred on our post. I knew from reading the *Stars and Stripes* newspaper that there were race riots in the States. On Saturday nights at the EM Club, the white boys and the black boys would always end up in big gang fights. Sometimes they would put on their helmets and get bunk adaptors and slug it out. We Indians and the Mexicans were upstairs watching the others fight. It was like we were a third party. As a result of the race riots, a lot of arrests were made by the MPs, and it seemed like they only arrested the blacks. I think the fights were a carryover from the race riots in the States.

After spending three Christmases, three New Year's Days, three Easters, and three Thanksgivings in Germany, I became really lonesome. One Christmas my mother had sent me a record with some Lakota music on it, and that really brought back memories of summertime at Pine Ridge when we went to the pow-wows and heard the drums beating all night. I was so lonesome, I decided to try and get an early release to go back to college. I wrote to Black Hills State College and they accepted me, but it was too late to get my early out.

One night right before I was discharged, I was down at the Luna Gardens drinking when, suddenly, for no apparent reason, I got sick and really vomited. The barmaid, Helda, came out and said, "What's wrong? Did you eat something to make you sick?"

I said, "No, I didn't. I can't understand why I'm sick; I've been drinking here almost every night for three years."

She stopped, looked at me, and said, "Yeah, I know. Maybe that's why you're sick: you drink too much."

I quickly denied it by declaring, "No, I can handle it. I'm OK."

Now when I stop and think back on that incident, maybe my body was telling me something; but at that time in Germany, I was too stubborn and ignorant to accept it. I know now that when a person passes out, it is the body's way of saying there is too much alcohol in it. If a person drinks too much, he or she can die from alcohol poisoning.

Well, the day came when the CQ (Company Quarterly) came by to give me my discharge orders. He said, "You have twenty-four hours to clear post."

"Twenty-four hours!" I exclaimed.

He answered, "Yeah, you're going home. You have twenty-four hours to clear post." Usually, a person gets a week, but I was given only twenty-four hours. Normally, guys would hold a little sale and sell their belongings. Heck, I had to give things away: my cuckoo clocks, my ski gear. I just had a big giveaway. But I was excited because I was going home.

Along with others who were leaving, we were put on the train to Bremerhaven, where we loaded on ship to go home. I had flown to Germany, but the army sent me home by ship. We were standing on the deck of the big ship, looking out as we were leaving port. Down below on the docks, an army band played "Auf Wiedersehen" and about six German women were standing down there waving goodbye to us. I think the U.S. Army paid them to wave to us because most of the Germans I had met hated GIs. To top everything off and increase that hatred even more, some of the GIs were throwing their leftover German coins at the women, saying, "Goodbye, you stupid Krauts. Here are your damn pfennigs."

It took us nine days to sail across the ocean. As we were going across the North Sea, we ran into a storm and the ship's crew said, "Button up the ship." That meant they pulled all the doors shut and tightened them closed with a big wheel on the door. There were sixty-foot waves going across the bow and the ship was just like a cork in the water. Everybody on board became sick. There was vomit smell everywhere. The stairways were made out of crate iron, so if somebody vomited upstairs, it fell all the way to the bottom floor. After a while, even if a person wasn't sick, just the smell on the entire ship made one sick.

I lucked out once again. The first sergeant of the ship happened to be a paratrooper. At the beginning of the trip, he called all the paratroopers up and gave us easy duty, mine being just to empty trash cans on the cabin class. One morning I said, "Hell, I'm not going to work today. I'm too short to work." ("too short" meaning a short-timer who has only a few days left in the army)

When I didn't report to work, the first sergeant called me in and ordered, "You're still in the army, soldier. Now I'm going to have to put you on KP. Report to KP."

Reporting there, I found that the cooks had too many guys on KP already. I told them that the first sergeant said I had be there anyway. They said, "All right, go to the kitchen and find yourself a job."

I went into the bakery and said, "Let me help you." I got to work making pies, bread and cakes. It smelled good in there all day long, and I never did get sick from the vomit smell. We were in the storm for about two or two-and-a-half days, and it reached a point where we were serving only about twelve meals per day out of 1,000 on the ship. Everybody was sick.

I remember the army stockade chain gang, composed of only black soldiers. The army was sending them back to the States to serve their sentences. They were extremely sick because of having to ride in the front of the ship (the front of the ship bounces the most in a storm), but the MPs told them they needed to eat; otherwise, the dry heaves would make it worse on them.

I didn't know when we were getting close to America, but the merchant mariners who were on the ship did. One day, the seagulls were flying by, and the mariners said, "We're close to land."

"How can you tell?" I asked. "All I can see is water."

One of them replied, "Once you see seagulls, you're close to land." Sure enough, we were about two days away from land.

We pulled into New York Harbor and dropped anchor outside the city for the night. Very few people slept that night. The next morning we sailed in right past the Statue of Liberty. All the guys were really hollering and cheering. We landed in the Brooklyn Navy Yard and when the guys went down the gangplank, some of them were so glad to be home that they would fall down and kiss the ground.

The officials began moving us into a great-big elevator that could accommodate thirty people at a time. As they were moving us along, some of the guys started bellowing, "Moo, moo." Pretty soon, everybody was bellowing "moo" as they herded us into the elevators. They took us up and put us on the bus which took us over to Ft. Hamilton.

An hour later, I was discharged.

Glad to be Home

WELCOME HOME, SOLDIER BOY

After I was discharged, I took a cab to the Newark airport. It was the first time I had ever been in an American airport. I had never flown commercially before; I had flown only on military aircraft. I walked into the terminal and couldn't get over the number of airlines there were. I went up to the first one I saw and said, "I want to go to Rapid City, South Dakota."

The agent said, "We don't fly there." That got me thinking, "Which airline should I take?"

I saw one identified as Northwest Orient Airlines. I went over and asked if they went to Rapid City and was told, "Well, we can get you to Minneapolis, then connect you into Sioux Falls." I had a cousin, Don Wade, in Sioux Falls, so I agreed to the plan. When I arrived, I called him and he came and picked me up. The next morning he was going to take me to the bus depot, but the bus didn't leave for western South Dakota until 4:00 in the afternoon. I said, "Take me out to the highway and I'll hitchhike." (This was before the interstate was even built.)

Don asked, "Are you sure?"

"Yes, I'm wearing my uniform. People will pick me up. I'll be home by 4:00," I assured him.

By 4:00 that afternoon, I was in Kadoka, a border town to the reservation. As I left the small town, a carload of Oglalas pulled up. They were drinking wine and said, "Welcome home, soldier boy." They picked me up and we drank all the way to Interior. I got to Interior and caught a ride to Wanblee, where Virgil Randall, whom I had been in the paratroopers with, lived. When we arrived, I asked him to give me a ride home.

By the time I arrived home, I was so under the influence of alcohol, I could barely stand up. We pulled up to the house and it didn't even look like the same house. The trees had grown up, the house appeared to have changed. I wasn't even sure it *was* the same house. I looked to see if Dad's name was on the front: it was. Then I knew it was the right house. I opened the door and went in. My mom peeked out around the corner from the kitchen. When she saw it was me, she screamed, came running, and grabbed me. I was so drunk, we both fell down. I passed out right there and woke up a couple hours later, my folks sitting there waiting for me to wake up. That was my welcome home.

My brother, Pānk, was working at Fort Wingate, New Mexico at that time, and I wanted to see him. My buddy, Lou Tyon, and I jumped on the train and went to Denver. From Denver, we took the bus to Gallup, New Mexico. My brother met us there, and we stayed with him for six months. First, I just partied around Gallup. Then I tried to get a job, but the only ones I could find were as a gas station attendant

104

or working in the dormitory--mediocre jobs. I said to myself, "I'm smarter than this. I'm going back to college and try one more time."

That summer while waiting to go back to Black Hills State College, I went home to Pine Ridge to prepare for my return to college. I was looking for farm labor, any kind of work to earn a little bit of money. I noticed that many farmers now owned hay balers, which, of course, cut down on the need for as much human labor as before. The farm equipment being produced at that time was making work obsolete. Work, therefore, was becoming harder and harder to find.

One day, the BIA sent a notice out from their building that they were looking for people to fight forest fires. In those days, when the U.S. Forest Service came down to the reservation to get people to fight forest fires, all one had to do was get on a bus and go. There was no test, no physical exam or anything. Therefore, when I saw the notice for forest firefighters, I grabbed my jacket, quickly ran down and got on the bus. We drove all night long to reach the location of the fire. We got there early in the morning and pulled into base camp just as breakfast was being served. At the same time we arrived, a couple of truckloads of forest firefighters were also just coming in for breakfast. It was like a mad rush. The Indians were running for the chow line, and the firefighters were running for the chow line too. We hadn't even fought a fire yet, but we were worried about eating breakfast.

We put the fire out relatively fast, but while we were fighting it, the wind had shifted, and all the smoke was coming back toward us. Everyone on the fire line threw their shovels down and started running. I said, "I'm not going to run. I'm a paratrooper. I'm going to stay here and fight this fire." I stayed there, but the smoke became so thick, I couldn't breathe. I crouched down low, then decided I'd better leave. I threw my shovel down and suddenly realized I didn't know which was to run because the smoke was everywhere. Because I knew the wind had changed directions, I started going with it. Pretty soon, I was running out of breath. I began to get scared and was right on the verge of panicking. I was thinking, "What am I going to do?" Just then, the wind shifted and blew the smoke away. I felt very relieved.

That evening, we were staying up to put out the smudge pots. The weather got very cold, and some of the boys started throwing wood back on the fire to warm themselves up. That really tickled me: here we were, out attempting to put the fire out, and they were trying to build up the fire so they could keep warm.

Firefighter

I went to college with GI Bill money. The BIA wouldn't help me any longer because a person can get money from only one government source. I really tried hard when I returned to college, and I surprised myself by getting a "B" average the first semester. But then, the previous years I had gone to school, my grades were so low that I was required to repeat many courses. It was my fourth year, and my mother asked me if I was going to graduate. I said no, that I had to take a lot of courses over. I was a senior for two years.

In order to student teach, I had to get a "C" average. I needed a "B" in a particular course to make the needed average. I asked the professor what kind of grade I was going to get. When he wanted to know why, I told him I needed a "B" in order to get a "C" average so I could qualify to student teach. When the grades came out, he had given me an "A." I think that's the only "A" I received in college. I'll never forget how Dr. Edwards helped me qualify to student teach.

My last year at college, I married a Hopi Indian girl from Arizona whom I had met when I was visiting my brother, Pānk, the previous year. One could probably could call it a shotgun wedding. We had to get married and that spring, our first daughter, Cindy was born. Because my wife complained about my drinking, I decided to go see a priest. I approached him and told him I had problems, but he tried to avoid me. I remember the expression on his face; it was like "helplessness." I guess the priests are not taught how to deal with alcohol and domestic problems. I left with no help, not even a referral where I could go for help, so I just returned to my old habits.

Once I finished college, I taught at Fort Wingate, New Mexico for four years at a BIA school for Navajo children. The first year I taught metal shop, and the other three-- photography, printing, and audio-visual. Because many of the students in the school did not speak English fluently, I used a method of picking out the four top students as team leaders to translate my instruction to each of four groups into which I had divided the classes.

I also asked students to do projects in my classes that were applicable to their culture. In the metal shop class, some made wood-burning stoves, branding irons, belt buckles, and spurs; one student even made a stock rack for his pickup. Six students in my photography class entered a national contest sponsored by Kodak. At first, the students questioned my asking them to take pictures that portrayed life around their homes. Being so accustomed to seeing such things as a goat standing on its hind legs, a sheep dip, goats in trees, they didn't find anything out of the ordinary in these scenes. It turned out that all six students' photos won in the Kodak contest.

While in the southwest, I had an opportunity to see some ancient American Indian cultures in action, the Navajo and the Hopi. A look at these traditional cultures only refueled my desire to study my own history and culture, begun when I met the Indian hobbyist in Germany.

During my teaching at Fort Wingate, I joined an independent basketball team by the name of "Eddie's Falcons." There was an all-Indian basketball league on the Navajo reservation, which I joined. Three of us were from South Dakota--my brother, Jim Bill, Delaine Provost, and I; three from Oklahoma--Marshal Thompson, Jack Pate, and Bill Nuttle; and a couple of Navajo boys--Stan Milford and Pete Sarimento. Even though there were only eight of us on the team, we won the Navajo League each of the four years I played with them. In four years, we lost only four games. Just to go to a game, we sometimes had to travel 200 miles in one evening.

In 1970, I was selected to be on an educational panel at the National Congress of American Indians. Their annual conference was held in Anchorage, Alaska that year. Since NCAI would not pay for anybody to attend the conference, I had to raise my own travel and expense money. After meeting with several organizations and getting no help, I decided to ask the local Catholic priest in Gallup, New Mexico. After I explained my situation to him, he turned around, opened his safe, took out a stack of hundred-dollar bills, counted out five, and gave them to me. I thanked him and left. I often wondered where he got so much money.

For the next four years, I started attending educational conferences; but, when I went to them, I didn't attend any meetings. I just went to party.

The National Indian Education Association was holding its annual conference in Milwaukee in 1972. One evening, it seemed like the entire conference delegation was partying in the halls of the hotel. Dan Honani, a member of the NIEA Board at that time, was walking up and down the halls begging the Indian delegates to return to their rooms.

At another NIEA conference, a group of us Lakota Sioux were drinking and telling stories in a hotel suite. I suddenly got an idea about how to raise drinking money for myself. I pulled out my tape recorder and put on a trick song, then challenged everyone in the room to a dance contest. I passed a hat around for monetary donations. The winner of the contest would receive the donations as his prize. Everyone had a good laugh because people who usually didn't Indian dance were doing so. Their actions were hilarious! The participants were gradually disqualified until there were only two--Manny Moran and myself. Of course, I won because the tapes were mine. I knew the songs!

In 1972, Little Crow, who was the Chief of the Mdewa-kantonwan Santee during the eight-week war in Minnesota, was finally buried at Flandreau, South Dakota. He was killed in 1863, and he was buried in 1972--109 years after he was killed. When he was killed, his remains were put on display at the State Capitol in Minnesota. Eventually, they ended up with the State Historical Society. My great-uncle, Jessie Wakeman, my mother's uncle, was the grandson of Little Crow. He had tried for years and years to get the remains returned, but to no avail. It was in 1972 that a friend of mine named David Beaulieu, whom I had met at the University of Minnesota when I was attending school there, was working for WCCO, a television station in Minneapolis. The station began a documentary on Little Crow. They were going to expose the State Historical Society of Minnesota for not releasing Little Crow's remains to his relatives. As soon as the Historical Society found out about the documentary, they agreed to give the remains to Uncle Jessie, also agreeing to transport the remains to Flandreau, and pay for the monument for his gravesite. Fewer than ten people went to the burial, held in September of 1972. Uncle Jessie was there, and my grandma and my mother. Shortly after that, Uncle Jessie died. I guess he was just waiting to get the remains of Little Crow returned and buried. Once that was accomplished, he went on to the spirit world himself. On the gravestone of Little Crow was engraved his Indian name, "*Ta-Oyate Duta*" (His Red People) and the following: "Therefore I will die with you." (See Introduction for reference to the eight-week war of 1862.)

In 1973, the American Indian Movement had gone into Wounded Knee, South Dakota in protest of Indian treatment on the reservation. AIM went in and took over the store. They ransacked the museum there and burned it down, and then they decided to protest. They stayed and occupied the store. The Indian police were called in and then, eventually, the FBI came. The event made the news headlines all over the nation. I was living in Phoenix at the time, working as an administrative intern at Cook Theological School. One weekend I was in an Indian bar in downtown Phoenix. I was drinking and had a little bit too much under the belt. I started bragging to the people in the bar that there were about ten of us paratroopers who were going to fly up there to Wounded Knee and jump in. We had reinforcements that we were taking to help AIM. Well, I didn't think anything of it; it was just drunk talk. The next day, though, the FBI was knocking on my door. They knew my name and everything about me. I don't know how they got the information, but they wanted to know how many airplanes we had, what kind of arms we had, how many paratroopers. I said, "Hey, wait a minute, that was all just drunk talk down in the bar." They listened to my explanation and didn't bother me any more. But I noticed that around town in the Indian bars--there are about five Indian bars in Phoenix--there were new bartenders. I observed one at a place where my friends and I usually went; he was really eavesdropping on everything that went on. I just figured he was an FBI agent planted in the Indian bar to keep their eyes open on what was happening with the AIM situation.

In 1974, I was working in South Dakota as Agency Superintendent of Education at Lower Brule and in the same year, I organized the Lakota Nation Trades Fair. A trades fair such as this had not been held in over 100 years. Previous to that time at the Lakota Wacipi (dance), the emphasis had been on the fancy feather dance and fancy shawl dance contests. As a contrast at this fair, however, we emphasized traditional dancing and traditional arts and crafts as being more important than modern fancy dancing.

During this time in my life, my Hopi wife was trying to force me to stop my drinking, but her controlling techniques only caused me to resist and drink more. Later that same year, 1974, our marriage ended in a divorce. I resigned my Superintendency and moved to Denver.

By 1975, my drinking had increased. The girl I was living with in Denver didn't want me to drink. She told me if I wanted to continue drinking, that was fine with her, but she would leave if I continued. Because I didn't want her to leave, I quit drinking. Well, that may sound easy, but the fact was, I had a hard time fighting temptation once I decided to quit drinking. As an example: once, temptation came and I finally broke down. I went to the liquor store and got a bottle. Then I thought, "Where am I going to drink this?" I drove to the park, but some people were there. Since I didn't want them to see me drinking, I decided to put the bottle of liquor in the trash can and come back later to drink it. Well, as soon as I told myself that I'd come back later and drink it, the temptation vanished. (I often wonder whatever happened to that bottle in the trash can.) This technique, in Lakota philosophy and thought, is called walking the Red Road. I had to learn from personal example that when temptation came, to say, "Later." A person can say to oneself, "I'll drink later." I used this technique more than once to help me gain sobriety.

Alcoholic Realization

My girlfriend and I were married in 1975, and we moved to Arizona, where I became the head of a BIA boarding school. I wanted to prove to myself that I could manage a school. Since I had left the Superintendency in South Dakota, I hadn't really proved to myself whether I could run a school or not. The Arizona school had an enrollment of 600 students. While there, I started the first education component for handicapped children on the Navajo Reservation.

During the time we were in Arizona, my wife, Dorothy, and I returned to South Dakota to help officiate the Second Annual Lakota Nation Trades Fair, of which my brother, Hep, and Doug White Bull were now the leaders. We left for Arizona as soon as the fair was over, driving all night and all the next day. At about 9:00 that evening, we were approaching the boarding school where I was employed and, all of a sudden, two buffalo jumped out and ran in front of the van. I checked our speed and we were going about sixty miles an hour. The buffalo continued running in front of us for about ten seconds and then they veered off to the right and disappeared into the night. This might not be so strange if it weren't for the fact that there are no buffalo in the area! My wife's father, Ike Brave Eagle, who was with us, told us to take some food, go out and pray, then make a food offering to the spirits. This we did.

That following year, my wife and I returned to South Dakota where I was employed with the Rosebud Sioux tribe as the Head of Education. That's when I learned how petty tribal politics can be. It seemed as though tribal officials' self-interest was more important than the priorities that should have been set for the entire tribe.

Sometimes, blocking tactics would be used. For example, we had to follow federal guidelines that required tribal council approval. We set up several meetings with the council, but no one ever showed up. We went ahead and completed the information as best we could, only to have tribal council members complain about who had authorized such information, claiming that no one had let them know about the meetings for their input.

We went to a ceremony to find out what I should do about the situation. The spirits told us to stay and deal with it, but I decided to leave. The day we were leaving, I loaded a U-Haul truck in 20° below zero temperatures. My wife remarked later that this was a very sad day for her because we had no jobs and no place to live. We stored our furniture with my folks and returned to Denver to look for work. I found a job with Boulder County and we moved into a one-room apartment.

My position at Boulder County was Housing Rehabilitation Specialist. Applicants who made less than $6,000 per year could qualify for a $5,000 grant to repair their homes. It was my job to verify the applicants' income and visit their homes to see who needed repair work the most.

I was shocked to see the extremely poor conditions the homes were in. Some had no plumbing, a few had no electricity. I thought to myself, "Heck, these houses are in worse shape than homes back on the reservation. People back home don't realize how lucky they really are."

116

In visiting with the owners, some would say to me, "I wish this were a loan. I sure hate taking money for nothing."

I would tell that person, "Look at it this way: every year you pay taxes, right?"

He would nod "yes."

"Then this grant money is the tax money you paid in."

He would respond, "I still don't feel good about it."

I then reminded the person about the large amounts of tax money being spent on countries overseas. "It's about time our government helps us." After listening to my explanations, the homeowners felt better about receiving the grant money.

That summer my former wife appeared and dropped off our four children, Cindy, Sandy, Hok and Fred. With my present wife, Dorothy, her two children from a previous marriage, the twins Dawn and Dana, and myself, we had a total of eight people living in a one-room apartment, but we managed. Dorothy was doing consultant work at the Community College of Denver, and one day an Indian lady told her she was on the College Board, which was looking for a qualified person for the position of Director of Student Supplemental Services. I applied and was hired. I felt like I was the College's token Indian. My office was on the first floor beside the main entrance. But I remained at the Community College of Denver for three years.

While living in Denver and working at the Community College, Dorothy and I decided to buy a home. We bought one under the GI bill, my first homeowner experience. I paid about $800 a year in taxes and had to pay for my own water and garbage pick-up. The garbage truck wouldn't pick up everything, just certain items. Homeowners had to haul larger items to the dump themselves. I'll always remember going to the dump. It cost $3.00 just to go in. Back home on the reservation, we'd just take our garbage and throw it in the pit, never thinking anything about it. Being actively involved really made me think about my garbage, my waste, and my water. A person starts thinking about conservation and related matters. Thus, being a homeowner really opened my eyes to the utilization of taxes and tax monies. I learned that my tax money was used for the following: Police Department, Fire Department, road maintenance, sewer and water, parks, community development, and senior citizen programs.

My oldest son, Hok, was living with us while we were in the new house in Denver. He was going to school with the twins. One day when they were riding home on the bus, two older boys spit on him and called him a dirty Indian. Well, the twins, his step-sisters, jumped up and tore into those older boys. (They were close to the same age as the twins.) The twins came home very excited, telling about what the boys had done on the bus and how they had chased them off.

My children stayed with me less than a year when my former wife wanted them back. They decided to go with her, except for Hok. My children had enjoyed their stay with us. It was like we were the "Brady Bunch." Hok's mother, I feel, bribed him into returning to her, telling him she would buy him a new bike if he came back.

Right after my children returned to their mother, my second oldest daughter, Sandy, had a dream of me dying, which repeated itself three times. Anyone who has studied dreams knows that if a dream recurs, it's a dream of urgency. She phoned me and said she was worried. She wanted to warn me about the dream and to inquire about my health. I said I was all right and that she was not to worry, but the dream interested me, so I studied it. I realized that she was at the point of puberty when she had the dream. I learned that when a person dreams of anything or anyone dying, it means that there is going to be a rebirth. The interpretation of the dream, therefore, was that in reaching puberty, Sandy had a new image of her dad and the old image was dying away. That's what the dream was telling her. When I called her and told her what the dream meant, she felt relieved.

One day a Wild West Show came to town while we were living in Denver. The organizers called the Indian Center looking for Indians to be part of the show. They wanted participants to have their own outfits for the two-shows-a-day performances. My brother-in-law, Sonny, and I went down, and they hired us for the Wild West Show. Well, when we got there, they said, "Go over to the corral and pick yourself out a horse. You're going to ride in the grand entry." We roped out a horse, saddled up, and rode in the grand entry.

We came back and were going to turn the horse loose when the owner came over and said, "No, don't turn your horse out yet. You guys have to attack the wagon train."

We said, "What!"

He said, "Go over there to the van and get yourself a repeating rifle with blanks."

Part of the show called for a covered wagon to drive out for us to attack, shooting blanks at the pioneers. Then Buffalo Bill and some soldiers would come out and chase us off. That was the plan. Well, we attacked the wagon train, shooting and whooping and hollering, putting on a good show. Buffalo Bill suddenly came riding out with his soldiers, who started shooting at us. A couple of the soldiers hollered at us, "Fall dead, Indian, fall dead!"

Wild West Show

I said, "Hell no, you fall dead." I guess that was a real turning point for us Indians. We didn't want to fall dead any longer. The second day, we kept some of the Indian boys back. After the soldiers started shooting at the Indians who were attacking the wagon train, then the other Indians jumped out from behind the bleachers. They had an ambush waiting for the soldiers. Boy, the owner of the Wild West Show got angry because the Indians were not supposed to win!

While at CCD (Community College of Denver), I used to teach Wednesday evenings at Littleton Federal Prison. Every week when I went there, the officials ran me through security and then I would go through three different iron doors. When I got inside, all the prisoners would be in line to go to their classes. The blacks were lined up in one line, Mexicans in another, Indians in their line, and the white boys lined up for their class. I remember the Indian guys teasing each other. They'd turn around, look at each other and say, "Hey, you're in the wrong line; the *Hasapa* line is over there."

I taught Native American History and Culture to Native American inmates at the prison. I received no pay, but I felt that a lot of these Indian boys needed to understand their history and culture so they could gain a greater sense of identity to help them continue on in life.

About 95% of these Indian boys were in prison because of a crime committed under the influence of alcohol. Nearly all of the 95% didn't remember their crime because they were so drunk. Later, I learned that when one becomes drunk to the point where one loses control of oneself, that person has opened himself or herself to evil spirits. Personally, I feel that this is what had happened with these boys in prison. Therefore, it seemed to me that they needed some sort of identity to cope with the problems at home so they wouldn't have to rely on the alcohol as much.

Several boys asked me to speak for them at their parole hearings. This I did, and the boys would usually be given a release date. As the date came closer, the boys started counting the days, some even making short-timer sticks. Some of them would get into trouble and then their release would be canceled. The prison officials' explanation was that because these boys did not want to face the outside world, they deliberately got into trouble so they could remain in prison. I never believed this, but couldn't refute it. It wasn't until I had the following experience that I was able to understand these short-timer feelings.

I was on a Vision Quest with Dawson No Horse as the Medicine Man Helper. When he put me on the hill, he told me, "I'll be back at 6:00 p.m. on the third day to take you down." The third day was very hard. I decided to make a sundial in the sand and count the hours until Dawson would come and take me down. When I began counting the time, the harder it was to stay up there.

Just as I decided to quit and walk down on my own, I took one more look at my sundial and said to myself, "What am I doing watching this clock?" I erased my sundial clock in the sand and said to myself, "Dawson will come when he comes." As soon as I said this to myself, the temptation to leave the hill left me and I was able to complete my Vision Quest. Later, as with a previously-mentioned realization, I understood this concept to be the Red Road approach. I hope that this experience can help people in similar situations--other short-timers--to deal more effectively in the future to make it through their last days in prison.

The first time I went on the hill (Vision Quest), I dreamed that three spirits came to visit me. They had no faces and they had on long white robes as they flew in and stood in front of me. I could not recognize them, but I received a really good feeling with their presence. One stood in front of the other two, who were behind his shoulders at each side. The one in front spoke to me, saying, "We want to be able to communicate with you while you're here on earth." I recalled the serpent vision that I had in the Badlands years before. Now these three spirits had come to me and said they wanted to communicate with me from the other side. I felt this dream, then, only verified the idea of transcendence and communication with the unconscious mind described by Dr. Jung--what the serpent vision was all about.

I told Dawson about this dream. He looked at me a short time, then said, "Study it, Chuck, don't grab it and run," meaning there's a danger when one immediately thinks he or she is special, spiritual or sacred on the basis of one dream or vision. A medicine person later commented to me that nowadays, too many people are running back to the pipe instead of walking toward it.

While living there in Denver, I would go back to the reservation to go hunting. On the Pine Ridge Reservation, I got an elk hunting license. When I was a kid, no license was required; anyone could just go hunting. But now the tribe has established a ranger system and has started issuing licenses.

The first year I went back, I shot an elk with one shot right through the heart. It was kind of surprising. I just aimed at the elk and shot. When we butchered it, we saw that the shot had gone directly through the heart.

The second year when I went back for hunting, I was bragging to everybody that all I needed was just one bullet. My dad said, "Here, you'd better take a clip; you're going to need more than one bullet." Marvin Ghost Bear and I were walking out across the canyon and, all of a sudden, some elk appeared down at the bottom of the canyon. We waited until they got a little bit closer, and then I opened up. Those elk took off up the other side of the canyon. I shot and hit one in the front leg. It staggered and when the others got to the top of the hill, they ran over it and out of sight. The one I had shot stopped and was just standing there, so I shot him again. This time I hit him in the rear leg. Now he had only two legs, but he hobbled out of sight over the hill.

We quickly jumped in a pickup truck and drove all the way around the hill to find the wounded elk. He was sitting at the edge of a cliff. I had used up my whole clip and had no bullets left. I said, "I'll walk over and slit his throat." As I went to do so, he tried to get up. When I looked at him, he looked right at me. I looked directly into his eyes and I'll never forget that look he returned to me. It was like he was scared and was trying to say something but couldn't. I wasn't able to slit his throat. It was easy to shoot him with a gun from a distance, but when I stood there over him, I felt sorry for him. The guide we had with us that day slit the animal's throat.

After that, I just gave up hunting. I sold my rifle and I've never gone hunting since. Later, I learned that in traditional times when one planned to hunt one's brother, the elk, it was proper to hold a ceremony before the hunt.

Elk Killer

One day, my brother-in-law, Sonny, came to Dorothy and me and asked us to help him. His girlfriend, who had a child from him, had died in a car accident. He asked us to take his three-week-old son and raise him. We kept the boy for a year, and then the father wanted him back. So the little boy went back to his dad. The twins were very upset because they had gotten attached to him. For my part, I was the one to change his diaper each morning and give him his bottle. Then we would watch the morning news on TV together.

At the Sun Dance in 1981 at Frank Fools Crow's place, I decided to pull seven buffalo skulls for Dawson No Horse, who had become sick with cancer. The skin on my back was pinched and an incision made for a cherrywood skewer to go through. A rope was then tied to the inserted skewer and the seven buffalo skulls attached to the end of the rope. I was then led to the edge of the sacred circle where I was to pull the skulls. Before I started, Jim Dubray, one of Dawson's helpers, came up, put his hands on my head, and prayed. As I began to pull the skulls, it felt like every muscle in my face and upper torso was being drawn backward. The pain was tremendous! I began to cry and, at the same time, I was praying for Dawson. About halfway around the circle, I had a vision of Christ walking beside me, dragging a giant cross. He was suffering with me as we walked together. I did not tell anybody about this for two years because I did not understand what Christ was doing in the Sun Dance. I was comforted with the fact, though, that the Bible says, "Whenever two or three are gathered together in my name, there I am in the midst of them."

Sun Dance Vision

In 1982 in Regina, Saskatchewan, I was conducting a workshop on the original teachings of the Red Man. It was an international meeting of indigenous peoples. I used slides in my presentation and, naturally, it was dark in the room. I noticed a mist in the projector's light, floating around to my front left side, and I thought somebody was smoking in the room. It seemed to be kind of a smoky mist. Well, after my presentation when I turned on the lights, I saw that no one was smoking. When I finished, everybody left except one woman, who came up to me and said, "I don't know if you realize it or not, but there was a cloud that surrounded you while you were talking." She continued, "Standing in that cloud was a spirit. It was the Christ spirit that was standing with you while you were giving that presentation." I thanked her and never really thought about it after that. I didn't know what to think, I just let it be. But I'll always remember what she said.

One weekend when I was living there in Denver, I decided to go up into the mountains and get some tipi poles. I got a permit from the park service, went up to the area they had pointed out, and began cutting tipi poles. Even before noon, people started pulling in with their chainsaws, and they were cutting trees. The woods were filled with the sound of chainsaws buzzing! All I had was an axe to cut down my poles. Suddenly, it got quiet, and I looked around. (I had long hair in braids at the time.) I became aware that all these loggers with their chainsaws had noticed that an Indian was in the forest. One by one, they came over; one guy offered me a sandwich, another offered me a drink. They'd come over with coffee and they'd visit. They'd say, "You know, it's a shame what the people are doing to the forest. You guys had the right idea." And they would go on and on. The way they talked, it was like somebody else was cutting down the forest, but they were the ones with chainsaws! It seemed like they couldn't see themselves.

I started trimming the tipi poles with a hatchet. Well, when I hit one, the hatchet glanced off and struck my other hand right across my thumb, leaving a big gash. Boy, I really started bleeding! I went to the van, got a handkerchief, and tied it very tightly around my hand to stop the bleeding. Then I went back to trimming the trees. I told my wife later that I couldn't let all those people in the forest know that the Indian was hurt because they were all watching me. They thought I knew was I was doing. I just kept chopping away and trimming up my poles. I had to load the poles with one hand because I couldn't even grip with the injured hand. That's what really tickled me--the urban Indian got hurt chopping tipi poles.

While I was working at Leupp Boarding School in Arizona, I joined the pow-wow dance circuit. I started competing as a traditional dance contestant. When I won a few dance contests, I really got the contest bug. I began traveling great distances just to get into dance contests.

Dorothy and I went to a pow-wow in Lame Deer, Montana one Fourth of July when we were living in Denver. The previous year, I had taken first place in the men's traditional dance contest, and I wanted to return to try for the prize again. At the pow-wow, I came upon Dorothy talking to a man. I questioned her about it, and the more I questioned, the more angry I became. Soon, I started to rough her up. She called for the police and had me thrown in jail for disorderly conduct.

That night, I had a lot of time to think about what I had done. Dorothy had said that the man was just an old schoolmate and that was all.

The next morning, the jailer came around asking if anyone knew how to cook. The cook hadn't shown up for work, and the jailer needed someone to cook breakfast. I quickly shouted, "I'm a cook. I cooked in the army for three years." He let me out to cook breakfast. I boiled up coffee and oatmeal. I threw some raisins in the oatmeal and baked some biscuits. Then I fed the prisoners. They said it was the best breakfast they had ever had. I wondered if they were pulling my leg because I was never a cook in the army. I just made up the story to get on trustee status.

Once on trustee status, I began talking with the jailer about speaking for me to the judge. I told him I wasn't thrown in for drinking, only for disorderly conduct. I also mentioned that I was a contestant in the dance contest and I needed to make grand entry at 1:00 p.m. to stay in the running. When the judge came, the jailer spoke on my behalf. The judge asked me, "How much money do you have?"

"Ten dollars," I replied.

He fined me $10 and said, "Get out of here. I don't want to see you back here again."

I went back to camp and apologized to my wife. She was really surprised to see me and wanted to know how I had gotten out of jail. I told her how I did it, and I was glad because we didn't have any extra money to get me out of jail. I made grand entry and went on to win in the men's traditional dance contest. As a result of this experience, I had to learn how to deal with my insecurities. It took me a while, but now Dorothy is free to talk with whomever she wants.

It seemed like the more I won, the more I wanted to dance to try and win more money. Another time, there was a dance contest in Rosebud. Dorothy and I were having a hard time financially and didn't have the money to go, but I wanted to go; my ego wanted to go to the dance contest so badly that we finally did go. When we got to Rosebud from Denver, we had only $6.00 in our pockets between the two of us. I took second place in the dance contest, allowing us to fill up the gas tanks and eat steaks on the way home. That's what dance contests do to a person: they cause one to take risks by traveling great distances, just with the hope of winning.

Grass Dance Champ

Dance contests also cause a lot of jealousy. I can remember a boy from Canada who came to South Dakota. He had seen me dance and really admired my dancing. We got to visiting and he learned that I had written a book. He had a great deal of respect for me. Then he married into a local Lakota family, who were also dancers. His wife's father was a traditional dancer. All of a sudden, his attitude toward me changed. I wondered if it was because of the dance contest business.

Later, Dorothy and I got involved in running pow-wows ourselves. It was then that we realized how much unfairness there was in the dance contests. We learned how people would stack the judges. Even the scorekeepers changed scores to let their friends win. I just became so frustrated with the whole pow-wow scene that I quit contest dancing. "It's not the traditional way anyway," I told myself. I still go to pow-wows where I announce as an MC once in a while, and I still dance once in a while, but it's just at the traditional dances.

When I attended Western Colorado University to finish my Doctorate degree, I was sleeping in my van to save money. I would camp in a park in the mountains. One morning upon getting up, I loaded my pipe, prayed with it, then smoked it as I did whenever I had a chance. Well, it was at this point in my life that I was doing the origins of the Red Man presentations throughout the United States. People were really excited about the presentation, and I started to feel very good about that. This one particular morning after I had finished praying with my pipe, I put it back in my pipe bag and got out of the van. The sun was coming up and I was standing by a meadow. A hummingbird came up right in front of me and went to a flower. He got nectar out of the flower and then moved to another. As I raised my eyes, I saw that the meadow was plumb full of hummingbirds. Just then, it popped into my head that I wasn't the only one offering presentations on origins; there are a lot of people doing presentations. I felt that I was having a vision and what it meant to me was that I shouldn't get the big head because a lot of people were doing the same things. After I received my Doctorate, I left my job there at the community college and started my consultant business.

Doctorate Degree Completion

I started my own consultant firm because people were interested in the origins of the Red Man and in learning styles. (My doctorate research had led me into identification of learning styles for Native American children, and it was at this time I gave my first presentation on learning styles.)

I traveled around the country to Indian communities where I talked about learning styles, American Indian history and culture. I was a consultant for three years, during which I traveled to forty-four states and six Canadian provinces. Also during this time, the National Indian Education Association held their annual conference in Denver. I was on the working committee and was put in charge of organizing the workshops. I was able to invite many people who could talk about psychic phenomena, wholistic education, and different learning styles.

ORIGINS OF THE RED MAN

I would like to explain how I got involved in the search for my roots or origins. As mentioned before, my search actually began in Germany in 1962. That's when I became interested in my history and culture, which eventually led me into spiritualism. An interesting correspondence is that 1962 is when Alex Haley also started his search for his roots. The similarity, though, is that we started at the same time. Alex Haley's origin search went from contemporary times back to his tribe, whereas mine started from the tribe and went back to creation.

It was not organized research in the beginning, simply an interest I had. I sort of entered into it as a pastime. First, I read what I could get my hands on and then I started talking to elders. The research became more organized after an incident occurred in Denver in 1977.

One day my ankles became swollen and I couldn't walk. I went to the doctor and he didn't know what it was. He gave me some medication and I went home. After a week or two of taking medicine with no results, I decided that I would go see another doctor to get a second opinion. This physician, Dr. Fox, put me in the hospital for ten days for a thorough exam, after which he said he still didn't know what was wrong. "I know your ankles are swollen up and you can't walk. I'm sorry," he said. "In medical terminology, we call this a syndrome. You have a syndrome."

I told him, "If you can't do anything, then I'm going home and see a Yuwipi Man. He'll fix me up."

"Who?" he questioned. He wanted to ask more, but a wall was there, an invisible wall. Either his professional ethics or pride or something. He didn't ask me any more. I'm glad he didn't because I had never been to a Yuwipi ceremony, though I knew of them. Yuwipi is a healing ceremony that takes place on the reservation. It was actually jokingly that I told Dr. Fox I'd go home for the Yuwipi Man to help me. He said," Well, if there's someone at home who can help you, by all means, go." He was from England. (My feeling is that medical people from England may be more open to alternative healing than American doctors generally are.)

I asked my wife, after I got home, if she had ever been to a Yuwipi ceremony. She said, "That's how I grew up."

So I said, "All right, let's go." We loaded up the van and went to South Dakota for the Yuwipi ceremony. We went to a Medicine Man named Dawson Has No Horse. I was pleasantly surprised to find that he did not charge for his services. As a result of attending his ceremony, I was healed.

On the basis of my healing, I made a pledge to sun dance. This would be my *wopila* (thanksgiving) to the spirits for healing me. It was my first Sun Dance. On the third day in the late afternoon, I became extremely exhausted and overwhelmed from the heat. I was thinking to myself, "What am I doing out here?"

Just then, Dawson came up and said, "Nobody asked you to be out here."

I thought, "Yeah, he's right. I made a pledge to be here." Then I considered to myself, "How did he know what I was thinking?"

That really started me thinking about Lakota ceremonialism. I became more and more interested. I knew something significant was there, but I had no idea what. I had a lot of questions but no answers.

Right after my first Sun Dance, I returned to college to finish my Doctorate program and enrolled in a class called Jungian Psychology. I found many answers that I was looking for in this course. What Jung was talking about gave me some answers about traditional D/Lakota ceremonialism. The concept that really stuck with me was that of the collective unconscious. As a result of studying Jungian Psychology and comparing it to Native American ceremonialism, I found that what Jung called the collective unconscious is what Lakota people call the spirit world.

The study of psychology then led me to parapsychology. Once I got involved in parapsychology, the study of psychic phenomena and information from the collective unconscious, I did some comparisons and found creation stories from various sources to be almost identical. I took a psychic interpretation of Genesis that had come from the collective unconscious of a man named Edgar Cayce and compared that creation story with the Lakota creation story and the Hopi creation story. All three were so similar as to be nearly identical. That *really* got me interested in psychic phenomena and parapsychology.

One day, I was walking around in a bookstore and a book on the shelf that had a kind of glow around it. I was drawn to it. It turned out to be an account of Edgar Cayce's psychic readings on the island of Atlantis. I started reading about Atlantis, and the information sounded to me to be almost identical to the Dakota legends. We have a story of our people coming from a land under the water in the East. As I researched that story, I originally thought this land was under the Great Lakes area, but as I studied the culture and linguistics of the Dakota people, I found that there are thirty-six tribes which have the same language, and some of these tribes lived on the eastern seaboard--in present-day North Carolina. I got to checking on their oral history, and I discovered that they had the same oral history as we did-- that of coming from a land under the water in the east, or coming from an island in the east. I wondered, "Was this Atlantis that they were referring to?"

Then I came across another Jungian concept that he calls synchronicity. He said there is no such thing as chance. Everything that happens has a purpose, a reason and a plan. According to Jung, it would be synchronistic that I was looking for the origins of the D/Lakota people and also located information on this Atlantic island called Atlantis. I felt glad about the synchronicity of that. As I started study-ing Atlantis more, it dawned on me that if there was an island in the Atlantic at one time, and if people migrated east and west from Atlantis to Europe and America, then ancient people in America and ancient people in Europe could have similar cultures, architecture, languages. At that point, my research became organized. I began looking for comparisons and similarities which I found on both sides of the Atlantic.

Then, as I studied more of Edgar Cayce's readings, I was made aware of an island in the Pacific called Mu. The same concept existed about that island, that the people from Mu had migrated east and west to Asia into America. According to Cayce's psychic readings, the Red Man had appeared in Atlantis and in North America, and the island of Mu was inhabited by the Brown People. Brown People appeared in Mu and in South America. In studying the Hopi origin and legends, the Navajo origin and legends, and another tribe called the Yurok, I found that they, too, have stories and legends about an island in the Pacific.

Once again, I conducted organized research. I said, "Well, if the people from Mu migrated both ways, east and west, then there must be similarities from people in Asia and South America." I found identical cultures, linguistics, and architecture on both sides of the shores of the Pacific.

Cayce said that man appeared ten million years ago in five places simultaneously. In other words, the five races appeared in five places at the same time: Red Man in Atlantis and North America, Brown Man in Mu and South America, Black Man in the Sudan, Yellow Man in Gobi, and the White Man appeared in the Caspian and Carpathian Mountains in Europe.

In researching the origin of these legends, I came across a star origins story that many tribes have. We ourselves, the Lakota, say that we came from seven stars and appeared in the Black Hills. Seven stars (and the number seven itself) are sacred to us; that's the reason we have the seven sacred rites; that's the reason, in the beginning, we had seven tribes. Additional star information came from the book on a UFO connection, entitled *UFO... Contact from the Pleiades.* Pleiades is the name of a constellation of seven stars that exists in the heavens. This is exactly the place that many Native Americans say they originated from. Is that coincidence or is it synchronicity?

UFO...Contact from Pleiades

Also while studying the Edgar Cayce readings, I learned that there are three kinds of karma. (Karma is a cosmic law stating that whatever one does, it will come back to him or her, be it in this life or in a future one. (Karma, in Lakota, is called *okawige*.) For example, if one were a slave owner in a past life, that person could become the slave in the present life. Proponents of this law say that the difficulties one has in this life are a result of one's actions in a previous life.) The three are:

#1 - Individual karma
#2 - Group karma (example: the family)
#3 - National karma (example: tribe or nation)

Cayce said it is the development of the soul which is all-important. Each time one's soul returns to Earth, it will occupy a different body and experience a different set of circumstances. These circumstances are the result of karma. After the soul has experienced peace, patience, brotherly love, endurance of suffering, and balance and harmony, it is free to leave Earth's plane, for it has completed its evolutionary journey here on Earth. Cayce further recounted that a soul will experience an average of thirty lives before completing its evolutionary journey. Each soul, however, has free will, according to Cayce's teachings, and if one chooses to experience peace, patience, brotherly love, endurance of suffering, and balance and harmony for a period of two years, then that soul can complete its evolutionary journey in one lifetime.

Besides star-story origins, we also have a story about coming from underground, from the Wind Cave in the Black Hills. Many tribes have similar such stories. One day when I was in New Mexico, I had a dream about a kiva. The outside of the kiva represents the psyche of the human, and the lower part of the kiva is the same as the collective unconscious. I realized that stories of coming from the underground were allegorical stories representing man's emergence from the unconscious up into consciousness.

On the basis of my research, I identified places on the planet where cultural, architectural and linguistic similarities had occurred. (See my first book, *Mitakuye Oyasin/We are all Related* for further detail.) It was this information that I organized and put together into a formal slide presentation in a series of lectures entitled "Origins of the Red Man." I presented to various groups across the country and was gratified by how well-received the material was by Native American people. As a matter of fact, in 1980, at the National Indian Education Association annual conference in Dallas, Texas, 980 people attended my workshop on "Origins of the Red Man."

THE SPIRITS DID IT

While in Denver, we used to go to a sweat lodge at Daniels Park. Several of us--Harry Burke, Frank Sherwood, Duck Garnette and I--would gather together at least once a month to have a sweat ceremony. One of the boys we used to sweat with, named Melvin Running Horse, told me a story that I want to share. He said that back home, a Medicine Man was getting old and was going to choose one of his sons to take his place. He had two sons. One was a very nice, "goody-goody" boy who stayed home all the time. He never drank and never did anything wrong. He learned all the ceremonial songs and knew the proper etiquette of the ceremonies. The other boy ran around the country, drank, got in fights, ended up in jail, virtually did everything wrong. The family had a ceremony to decide which one of the boys this Medicine Man was going to pass his altar on to. The spirits picked Glete, the boy who did everything wrong. That always stuck in my mind, and I know that when people come to a Medicine Man for help, they have all kinds of problems relating to family, drinking, jail, and many other things. If such a person has no experience in these areas, then it would be very difficult to help individuals with problems. I thought maybe that's why the spirits picked the bad boy--because he had a world of experience that he could relate to the people who came to him for help.

In the 1983 blizzard in Denver, we got thirty-five inches of snow in twenty-four hours. It was just like the heavens dumped a bucket of snow on us. The whole city was paralyzed. It was at this time that I recognized that whenever there is a disaster like this, people really come out, put their differences aside, and help each other. It was really a good feeling after that blizzard. People were helping each other dig out. This brought to mind what the Bible states, that the next age will be a thousand years of peace. Does this mean that this age will end in disaster?

But this good feeling lasted only about a day-and-a-half. As soon as the roads were open again, as soon as the stores were open again, as soon as everything was back to normal, people seemed to return to their old bad habits of not acknowledging one another in the usual city way of living. My good feelings dissipated quickly.

When Reaganomics took hold in our country, consultant monies dried up, and I was forced to seek wage work once again. I applied for many jobs in the Denver area and went through a lot of interviews. I noticed that the people interviewing me would ask me questions that had nothing to do with the job. I felt I was just a token interviewee. Because of my education and race, they had given me an interview. The jobs that looked the most promising usually went to a Hispanic or Black. It was then I realized that American Indians don't have political clout in the cities.

Because the Bureau of Indian Affairs had Indian preference in hiring, I returned to the reservation to look for work. I was hired as Superintendent of Education for the Standing Rock Reservation in North and South Dakota. At first, it was a bit of a change, but growing up on a reservation, I had no problems adjusting. This job turned out to be fortunate for me because now I was able to put into action the wholistic education philosophy that I had been talking about during my consultant years.

That first winter at Standing Rock, I remember the twins had come home for Christmas from attending school in Kyle, SD. It was two days before Christmas and we loaded up the van and went to town to do our last-minute shopping for the "Blue Light Specials" at K-Mart. The temperature registered 97° below zero, with the wind chill, when we left for Bismarck. We had the heater in the van blowing full blast, yet only the windshield was defrosting. We had to dress in stocking caps and gloves and wrap up in blankets inside the van. I realized then why people warn others not to drive in that kind of weather, but if one does, they should always take food and blankets and remember the rule: in case something happens to you on the road, never leave your car.

The twins graduated from high school and applied for college. They were not eligible for any grants because of my income. Dorothy told the counselors that I was not the twins' blood father, but they said because the girls lived in my household, they would not qualify for education grants. Dorothy and I decided, then, that she should look for work. She was selected for jobs in Seattle and Washington, D.C. She decided to go to D.C. because she could stay with my brother and his family. After eight months there, she got transferred to Crow Creek Agency in Fort Thompson, SD as a BIA administrative officer. We were happy because now, instead of meeting once a month, Dorothy and I could be together every weekend.

One April, we decided to meet halfway between Fort Yates, ND and Fort Thompson. We had just completed our income tax forms and they had to be postmarked by April 15. We met in Hoven, SD on the afternoon of April 15, both reaching there about 4:00 p.m. We signed the forms and put them in the mail. After we mailed the forms, we decided to have supper together before we returned to our respective homes, even though it had started to snow heavily as I had driven into Hoven. We ate and then saw that the snowstorm had turned into a blizzard. Dorothy was afraid to drive home alone, so we checked into a motel, thinking we would leave for home the next morning. But the following morning, the snow was five feet deep, and the blizzard was on the increase.

We ended up being stranded there for three days. The cafe and grocery store downtown closed, but the motel owner sent us sandwiches and pop. The electricity went out the second evening, yet because the owner had an emergency generator for electricity, we had lights. The TV was out, but he sent over a VCR and a video of an old movie. I had also just received a video on Alkali Lake (the story of how the Sumash Tribe of British Columbia had gained sobriety) in the mail. We got it out of the van and watched the two videos over and over, about three times each. We had no books or newspapers and simply watched the videos repeatedly. Each time we watched the one on Alkali Lake, Dorothy would cry, and I would get a lump in my throat.

I was so impressed with the video that after the storm when I returned to work, I arranged for the Chalsee family (about whom the story revolves) to come to Fort Yates and talk to our staff, students and parents about their experiences. This was the first effort made by the school system to bring out an awareness of the severity of our alcohol problems on the Standing Rock Reservation.

People would frequently come to my home while I was working in Fort Yates as Superintendent, trying to hock or sell goods to me. First, they would usually relate a sad story to me, then tell me how much money they needed. I knew from previous experience as an administrator in a small community that I would be viewed as the community banker. This was due, largely, to the extremely high unemployment rate on the reseration and the fact that I was one of the highest-paid individuals living there. I tried to help as much as I could, but I needed to weigh each proposal very carefully. Still, there were occasions when people would take advantage of me and I would get "ripped off." For example, sometimes people borrowed money from me and never paid it back. Other times, items that could be sold were occasionally stolen from me.

While we were there at Standing Rock, I remember Dorothy telling one day that she was working in the kitchen and heard somebody call her from downstairs. The voice called, "Dorothy, Dorothy". She said she stopped her work and started to go downstairs. She suddenly remembered there was nobody downstairs. She became afraid and quickly ran upstairs. I began researching this type of incident and found the following story on the Edgar Cayce interpretations of the Bible: A man named Eli, according to Cayce, was training young men in the spiritual way. One of them was Samuel. One night Samuel heard his name called. He got up, he thinking it was Eli, his teacher. He went to Eli, but Eli said he hadn't called him and to go back to sleep. He did so and the voice called his name again. He got up and went to Eli again. Eli said, "No, I didn't call you. Go back to sleep." Samuel went to sleep again. The third time the voice called his name, he returned once again to Eli. Then the teacher knew what was happening. He told Samuel, "If this voice calls your name again, just say to it, 'Speak, Father, for I am your servant.'" Cayce remarked that it is not unusual for spiritual people to hear their name being called.

Shortly after this, my Grandmother Allen passed away, and three days after her death I had a dream in technicolor. My studies in psychology had led me to an interest in dream interpretation. The technicolor dream meant it was a powerful one. In the dream, my grandmother appeared. She called me and I followed her. She went down the hall and turned around a corner. I continued following her, but when I went around the corner, she was gone. I was looking for her everywhere when her voice said, "Don't worry, I'll always be with you." I interpreted this dream to mean that even though my grandmother had passed on, I shouldn't worry because her spirit would always be with me.

Grandma Allen grew up a Christian. She had a medicine bundle which was given to her by her Grandmother Standing Cloud. My grandmother never used it because she was a Christian. But Grandma Allen had a lot of respect for this bundle. Where some people might have just discarded it, she kept it in reverence, and passed it on to my mother. My mother took this bundle to Dawson No Horse and asked him what she should do with it. Dawson said it was a female medicine bundle and that my mother should pass it on to a female member of the family. The person in possession of such a bundle should pass it on, he said, when they have a dream to do so.

On August 16, 1987, Harmonic Convergence occurred. Carmen Taylor and I organized a conference in Denver to help make others aware of the shift in consciousness taking place on that date. Harmonic Convergence happened all over the world to usher in a new cycle according to the Aztec calendar that would start on August 16, 1987. Different sites held spiritual meetings and prayer sessions. We chose to host a conference to acknowledge the beginning of the new cycle. As one of the presenters, part of my talk was on the original teachings of the Red Man. I was referring to my mentor, Dawson No Horse, who had gotten me involved in Native American spirituality and had created an interest for me to where I went out seeking more and more. Afterwards, two ladies came up to me and said, "When you were up there talking about Dawson and Lakota spirituality, there was a man standing there beside you." One woman told me that she knew it was Dawson because she recognized him. The other one said who she saw was just an Indian man; she didn't know who he was. My thoughts immediately went back to the presentation I had given in Canada a few years before. The Christ spirit was in the cloud beside me at that time. This time, Dawson appeared. I had no idea that he was there. I was just doing the best I could. Not only did I feel really good about the women telling me what they had seen, but I also had good feelings about Harmonic Convergence. I discovered later in my research that Dawson's spirit was a part of the *Wakinyan Oyate*. The English term for Wakinyan Oyate is the Christ spirit.

When I finished giving my presentation, several people asked me, "Do you have anything in writing?"

I said, "No, that's not the traditional Indian way. The traditional way is to tell stories and share the information through presentations." Many commented that that was too bad because they felt that most of the material I covered during the conference was really valuable.

Some said, "When you tell it, you reach 100 people, but if you write it down you could reach 100,000 people." I thought about the positive response to my talk and decided that I'd go ahead and write it down. Thus, out of that conference eventually came the book, *Mitakuye Oyasin/We Are All Related*. What really helped me in writing the book was that my wife had to support her twin girls who were now in college. As mentioned previously, she chose a BIA job in

Washington, D.C. so she could transfer back out to a government agency close to home. When she did so, her work was just 180 miles from my place of employment. I would commute back and forth to her home on weekends and continued to live alone during the week. That's what gave me a lot of free time in the evenings to write the book. Dorothy had said that as soon as her girls finished college, she was moving back with me. When they graduated, she got a job where I was working and moved back home after four years of us living at separate locations.

A lot of preliminary work was required before my presentation could be made into a book. I made the decision to put my entire lecture series into book form and hired a typist to transcribe it from the tapes that had been made of the series. I reworked the transcription, rewriting and making changes where necessary for a reading audience. After that, an editor went through it for final manuscript editing for the book.

When I got the completed manuscript, I started contacting publishing companies. Four major companies agreed to publish the book for me, but they each said they could give me only an 8% royalty. I said, "Eight percent! Why?"

The question was the same from each publisher: "First of all, how many books have you written before?"

"None," I replied.

The next question, too, was the same: "Secondly, who are you? Nobody knows you. You're an unpublished, unknown author and therefore, that's all we can offer." I asked for an explanation of the 8% in dollars and cents. The idea didn't make much sense to me.

I was told, "Let's say we sell your book for $10. With our advertising and distribution costs, you'd get about $.20 a book."

"Wait a minute," I said, "You mean to tell me that if you sell five books, I get $1.00?"

The reply was, "Yes."

I said, "This book is twenty-eight years of my life. I can't give it to you guys for $.20 a book." I decided, therefore, against letting a publishing company do my book and made up my mind to self-publish it. I started contacting printers, got a pretty good deal from one in Denver, and let him print the book for me.

The next thing I had to do was to raise some money. Through my efforts, I came up with about $10,000 to print up the first batch of books. When I finally got the book printed, I decided to take it to bookstores for placement. The bookstore people would say, "Well, who are you?"

Very proudly, I'd say, "I'm the author."

They'd say, "We don't deal with authors. We deal only with wholesalers." Then I began contacting wholesalers or distributing companies. I'd say, "I have a book here and I'd like to know if you'd distribute it for me." Their response was, "Well, we have to have a committee read it. If we decide to distribute your book, we get 50% right off the top. If there's any advertisement, you'll have to pay additionally for it."

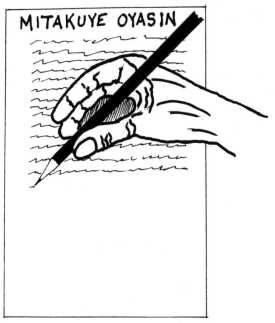

Native American Author

I really learned a great deal from getting into this book business. At last, I got the book out to several distributors, but since I had self-published, I needed to do my own marketing, my own sales, my own advertisement; I realized it was up to me to promote my own book.

It was a very long, hard journey becoming a book publisher. Now, *Mitakuye Oyasin* is in its fifth printing and it's only been out a little over two years. So I really feel good about the project.

In *Mitakuye Oyasin*, I made two predictions that have since come true. The first was that while I was in Holland, a dream told me that America had nothing to fear from

Russia. This dream occurred two years before the fall of the Berlin Wall and the disintegration of the Soviet empire. (*Mitakuye Oyasin*, p. 193)

The second prediction was that negative brain waves were involved in the depletion of the ozone layer. A report in the October 23, 1991 issue of the *Wall Street Journal* attributed "ozone depletion to sulphur particles from volcanoes." As stated in my book, volcanic activity is indirectly affected by negative brain wave energy. (*Mitakuye Oyasin*, pp. 114-115)

In 1987, I received a great surprise. The Hubert Humphrey Institute at the University of Minnesota was sending a delegation to the North Atlantic Treaty Organization to review and give a report on the status of NATO. They called and told me I had been selected if I would be willing to go. I said yes. I traveled to Brussels, Belgium with the delegation. My personal conclusion about NATO was that it was no longer needed. (See *Mitakuye Oyasin*, pp. 194-207 for greater detail about NATO trip.)

The National Indian Education Association held their annual conference in Bismarck during this time, and I had the great honor of being selected to give the keynote address on the second morning. I had just gotten back from Europe on the NATO trip. As part of my talk, I had decided to hold a ceremony. In the traditional Indian way, it is said that experience is the best teacher. one can lecture to people, but unless they experience the information for themselves, it doesn't really mean as much. Let me explain.

While I was in Canada doing consultant work, I came across a tribe living on the northern shore of Lake of the Woods. I told them about my great-great grandfather who had lived on an island in the Lake and asked them if they knew of him. They asked around, and someone confirmed, "Yes, the old people tell the story of a man who lived out there."

As we got to sharing stories, these Ojibwa people showed me their sacred drums. The drumkeeper took me into his house. He kept the drum in a separate room on an altar. He said, "We got this drum from the Sioux. The story is that we gave the Sioux a pipe, and they gave us this drum. They said that one day we would exchange the pipe and the drum back with one another, and we'd be at peace again." (The Sioux and Ojibwa--or Chippewa--were enemies in traditional times.)

I remembered that story, and I kept my eyes open for an old pipe when I was traveling around in South Dakota and Minnesota. I located a pipe that was almost 100 years old. I did not know if it was one of those sacred pipes that the Ojibwa had given us, but I was told it had come from the north. I offered the pipe to this group from the north shore of Lake of the Woods and invited them to the NIEA conference to receive it.

At the end of my keynote address, we had a Lakota drum group sing a ceremonial song, and we gave the Ojibwa people from Rat Portage Reserve this pipe. As the song was being sung, I felt a definite energy above the entire audience. I was really moved! I didn't realize the ceremony would be received so well. We told the audience about the drum and the pipe, that we did not know if this was the actual pipe from past times or not, but that we were willing to give these people our pipe in friendship.

By 1987, my efforts with wholistic education in Fort Yates were beginning to show. Our student scores were increasing, staff morale was up, people were getting excited about the wholistic education approach.

When I was Superintendent of Education at Standing Rock, I always remembered from my early childhood how I never had to go hungry because we had a garden, as spoken of earlier. We raised our own vegetables. Then later when I was in boarding school in Pine Ridge, we always had school gardens where we raised our own produce.

Because vendors from the surrounding reservation border towns wanted to provide dairy and vegetable services to the schools, they persuaded the government to start contracting these services to them. Consequently, the school gardens became obsolete.

The concept of school gardens from times past always stuck in my mind, and I discussed an idea with Bob Gipp, Assistant Superintendent at Fort Yates. I suggested that we ought to start up school gardens again as part of our wholistic education program. He liked the proposal, and we really pushed to have school gardens in our four BIA schools on the reservation. It was a fairly successful project. Standing Rock High School's garden turned out to be very successful. The tribe kept a tribal garden, and we had talked to the people in charge, who allowed us to have a plot of ground where we could plant. We bussed the kids out in the country where the plot was, and we planted our crop. We maintained the garden over the summer and in the fall, the kids would go out and harvest it--mainly potatoes. We did grow corn one season, but we generally just called our efforts the potato project school garden.

BIA education officials from the Office of Indian Education Programs (OIEP) came to Standing Rock one year, and we took them out to our school garden. They were really surprised at what we were doing and liked the idea. A result of our wholistic education program was that I was selected as one of the members of the National BIA Effective Schools Team, which promoted ideas such as ours. I felt a sense of pride that a concept I had initiated was finally being recognized.

One weekend, my wife and I had gone to Bismarck and were returning to Fort Yates. It was 10:30 in the evening, and we were going about 35 mph because that was the speed limit on the approach into Fort Yates. All of a sudden, we heard a bang. Somebody had run into us from the rear. It knocked us both backwards, breaking Dorothy's seat completely off and bending mine backwards. The car pushed us about twenty yards down the road until we stopped and I got out. The driver was drunk and didn't even stop. He just drove his car right around us and kept on going. Just then, the police were coming by. I signaled them and told them what had happened; they immediately chased the car. Come to find out later, the driver was a tribal employee who was influential with the tribe.

This man was never fined or punished in any way. We took the case to the tribal court, but nothing was done because in tribal court, the judge works for the tribal council, and the council wasn't willing to do anything to their own employee. The unfairness made the case seem like it had been handled in a kangaroo court. My wife and I are both non-tribal members with no voice in the Standing Rock tribal government. There was nothing we could do except reflect on how unfair the reservation tribal court system really is.

Dorothy and I were taken to the hospital right after the accident, and we had a lot of injuries. The next day, we went to a chiropractor, who adjusted our backs and necks. We were lucky because our seats had high backs and we didn't get whiplash, but we still had to get our necks and backs realigned. My wife's injuries continue to bother her to this day.

While I was working at Standing Rock, two men from the Zia Pueblo had gotten the school cafeteria contract. They were to provide meals at both the high school and the elementary school. I got to visit with these Pueblo men, and one day when we were having a sweat, I asked them if they wanted to come along and watch the door for us. They said, "What do you mean?" I explained to them what a sweat lodge ceremony was and what watching the door meant.

They both said, after hearing the explanation, "Well, we don't want to watch the door; we want to go in."

I said, "OK, if that's what you want to do." They came out to our sweat, participated in it, and really enjoyed it.

Later, they told me that at Zia Pueblo a long time ago, the people conducted sweats. They had talked to their grandpa who said that now, the use of the sweat lodge has gone by the wayside.

These two Pueblo men, Stanley and Larry Pino, who were cousins, invited me to Zia to do a presentation on wholistic education. While I was there, they said, "Let's have a sweat. Could you help us build one?" I helped them, of course, and after we got the lodge all set up, that night we went in for the first time to use the new sweat lodge. During the ceremony while we were praying, we could hear a buffalo snorting outside the lodge. The two Pino boys really got excited! Afterwards when we came out, there was nothing there. I explained to them that the buffalo spirits had come there to acknowledge what was happening, a very good sign. They felt thankful. Today, more and more people are returning to the old ways at Zia and using that sweat lodge.

The stress of being an administrator on the reservation finally started to take its toll on me. I reached a point where I was sleeping for ten or eleven hours a night but was still tired the next day.

One day my friend, Doug White Bull, came to visit me early in the evening, and I was already asleep. His son, Jon said to him, "What's wrong with Chuck?"

Doug replied, "Nothing. He's all right."

Johnny, not satisfied with the answer, persisted, "Come on, Dad, *tell me !* You know: tell me."

I mentioned this incident to my astrologer friend, Joe Osowski, who suggested I get a hair analysis test. So I did, and I found out that my body was metal toxic. I began a program to balance the minerals in my body and within three months, I was back to normal. But Doug's family and mine still have a good laugh when we talk about Johnny wanting to know what was wrong with me.

As a result of our wholistic education program on Standing Rock, the presentations I offered at the National Indian Education Association often inspired people to invite me to come to their schools and give presentations. One time as I was traveling to do a presentation on wholistic education programs, I had a layover in the Phoenix airport for about five hours. It just so happened that a pow-wow was going on that weekend, and my daughter, Cindy, was there, as well as my nieces, Kim and Kelly. They were all attending the pow-wow. I went out of the terminal building to get a cab so I could spend my time at the pow-wow visiting with my daughter and nieces. Well, the cab driver wanted $30. Just before I had gone to the cab, though, a guy with a limousine had asked, "Do you want to take a limousine?"

I had said no and when he asked where I was going, I said, "To a pow-wow."

He offered, "I'll take you there." In my mind, I thought the fare would be too high and that's why I had asked the taxicab driver how much he would charge to take me over there, wait a half-hour while I visited, and then bring me back. I felt the $30 he quoted me was too much and I started to leave.

At that moment, the limousine driver came running up and said, "How much did the cab driver want to charge you?"

I quickly understood the situation and responded, "He wanted $25."

"I'll do it for $20," the limousine driver countered.

I said, "You're on." I got into that big black limousine, we drove out to the Salt River Reservation where the pow-wow was being held, and went into the camping area. As we were driving around looking for my daughter and nieces, everybody was really gawking. "Who in the world would come to a pow-wow in a limousine?" I could almost hear people saying. With the dark windows, they couldn't see in.

I spotted my daughter and my nieces, so I stopped the limousine. Cindy and the girls were *really* looking at the limousine, as if to say, "Who in the heck is this pulling up to our camp?" I opened up the door and got out, and they all screamed and came running and jumped on me.

They said, "What are you doing in a limousine?" I told them it was a long story. That sort of tickled me: what kind of Indian goes to a pow-wow in a limousine?

My daughter, Sandy, stayed with me in Fort Yates one year and attended Standing Rock College. She joined the girls' basketball team and was soon taking trips with the team to games and tournaments. She began dating a boy named Terry Dogskin. A year later, I had another grand-daughter named Santee, who joined her cousin, Krystal, born the previous year to my daughter, Dana.

When my children started having babies, then I really knew what the concept of wisdom was about. Wisdom, as I understand it, is when one can reflect back on an experience or past knowledge, then make adjustments in present situations. Watching my children as parents, I could ponder my own parenthood and offer advice to my children.

In the winter of 1989, a friend of mine, Jody Luger, had just come home to Fort Yates for Christmas vacation from Alaska where he had been working. All the Sun dancers were welcoming him back with a sweat lodge ceremony that night. Right before we went into the lodge, the principal at the high school, Roman Weiler, had made a request that we have prayers for his son. I said we would. What had happened was that we had a championship basketball team, and his son, who played center for the team, had torn ligaments in his knee and wasn't able to play. He went to the doctor, and the doctor advised him that he could never play basketball again. That's why his dad requested prayers for him.

Earlier that year I had gone to a conference in Denver on psychic healing. I remembered an exercise that was taught. The instruction went that one needs to practice getting into the alpha brain wave pattern so that the spirit energy can enter one's mind to guide the healing. In my way of thinking, this is what happens in the sweat lodge. Participants are in the alpha state and the spirits can enter their mind and give them important information.

I didn't plan it at the time, but when we went into the sweat lodge, I decided to utilize Jody Luger with this psychic healing effort for Roman's son, Joe. Jody didn't know where Joe was hurt and that's why I decided to use him. The spirits told Jody where Joe's injuries were and what to do to help him. This was all done in the ceremony in a spiritual manner, and it was the spirits that brought out the information and instructed the healing. When I went back to work the next day, Roman Weiler told me his boy was able to walk, in spite of his sore knee. A week later, he was able to play basketball again. Roman said it was like a miracle. He asked, "What did you guys do in that sweat lodge?" I said that we hadn't done anything, we just had prayers. Whatever happened, the spirits did it.

In 1990, I received a call from a Soviet/American peace group. A peace conference was being held in the then-USSR. A lady who was the head of the spiritual component of the conference had read my book and asked me if I wanted to be part of their delegation to go to Moscow and speak on spirituality. I accepted.

In Russia, I was very fortunate to see it from a different perspective than most Americans might. Because I am Dakota Sioux, I was able to see Russia as a third party, observing American reactions to situations, as well as the Russian reaction. I was excited by what I saw in the Soviet Union. America could learn much from them--specifically the principles of equality, the work ethic, cooperation, and spiritual awakening.

St. Basil's Cathedral - Moscow, Russia

In the USSR, everybody works. Just within the hotel where I stayed, there were key ladies, doormen, coat checkers, telephone ladies, luggage men, and toilet checkers. Unemployment has been very low to non-existent there.

Salaries are not high and the jobs are menial, but everybody works. There is work, people are earning money, and they're proud. There's not much technology because technology eliminates jobs. There is some technology, naturally, but not on the scale it is here in America. Technology was created to benefit the masses, not to eliminate the masses.

Due to the lack of competition, there are no brand names in Russia. Most items are inexpensive, at least before the break-up of the Soviet Union. A telephone call anywhere in Russia costs two kopecks--one-sixteenth of a cent. A person can ride the subway all day for five kopecks--less than ¼ of a cent. Health care and education are free.

There is no welfare. In some places in the United States, people have been on welfare so long, they're starting to lose the work ethic. America needs to take a look at that concept. Cities need to create menial jobs so people work for a living instead of lying at home and waiting for a welfare check, then drinking it up as some in this country do.

Living expenses are low in Russia. Housing is very inexpensive, around $10 a month for an apartment. It doesn't matter if one is the superintendent of a school or the janitor--a person is allotted the same square footage according to the size of the family. The state also provides free pre-schools for working mothers. More and more mothers are starting to work, but it's not like here because the economy is different. (U.S. mothers who wish to work have to pay for their own day care.) I realize that conditions have changed and are changing even more rapidly since the break-up of the former Soviet Union. My observations are based on what I saw going on at the time I was there.

There are 120 different ethnic groups within the Russian population of 287 million, while in the U.S., more than 300 different ethnic groups exist among its 257 million people. The Soviet Union has dealt positively with its different ethnic groups, though there are presently many struggles within the individual countries centering on ethnic identity.

Our school system should address the need for positive ethnic identity. In the States, there's now a big push to have English be the only language of instruction. Such an attitude really has negative connotations for those raised with a different heritage and language from the mainstream. Minority students need to feel a sense of self-worth. It's one of the main ingredients for learning. Folk heritage is stressed within the schools in the USSR, which has very much endorsed that emphasis. There is pride in being a tribal member. Here in this country, by contrast, for years and years if a person was a tribal member, he or she was taught to shun his or her heritage.

In America, we pride ourselves on the Christian concept of equality. Yet, the moment one steps on a commercial airline, for example, the flight attendant asks if one is in first class, business class, or coach. In America, the profit motive has created a different type of class system.

Russian schools thrive within a cooperative atmosphere. Students sit two to a desk. Chairs are arranged in circles or U-shapes to encourage right-brain thinking, much like the wholistic methods used within the Standing Rock Agency schools. They are encouraged to work together rather than compete. Cooperation is the underlying premise in everything Russians do. They advocate equality, ethnic heritage, bicultural and bilingual education. They very much encourage schools to hire native teachers who can relate to the local ethnic groups. They teach languages other than Russian if another language predominates in the area. Russian students attend school six days a week, from 8:00 a.m. to 1:00 p.m. After dismissal, they go to their clubs for extracurricular activities such as gymnastics, chess, and computers. Because all education in the USSR has been free, Soviet students go on to universities or vocational schools after completing grades one through ten in public school. Military academies are difficult to get into because slots are reserved for officers' children.

In Russia, 52 percent of the population is atheist. Of the remaining 48 percent, one-half are Russian Orthodox and Roman Catholic, and the other half are Moslem, Buddhist or Jewish. I believe that because Russia is primarily atheist, the people have really delved into the paranormal, exploring such phenomena as Kirlian photography, mental telepathy, ESP, out-of-body experiences. Studies there, as in many other places in the world, have shown that there is an energy everywhere, and that it exists in everything. It can be called energy. Religious people call it God. Native Americans call it spirits. The terms are just different labels for the same phenomenon.

Not everything in Russia is perfect just as not everything in America is perfect. The current type of capitalism we have today isn't working. Our schools are set up to endorse our economic systems. One percent of the American people own fifty percent of the wealth. In the last eight years, that spread has greatly increased and the number of "have-nots" has greatly increased.

Communism also is not working, as we have dramatically seen in the break-up of the former Soviet Union. We need a blend. We need to look at the positive aspects of each system. Russia didn't wake up one day and see that our way is better, like our TV portrays. Russia is experiencing individuation by admitting her weaknesses and attempting to correct them. America is still in a state of denial about the cause of her problems.

What I observed when I was in Russia is that she is taking matters slowly, though recent changes there belie that fact. I saw a concern that a change toward capitalism could weaken the work ethic, that too much technology would cut down on the number of jobs. The changes, at that time, seemed to be coming slowly so that the positive parts could be analyzed and retained. My own thinking is that Russia's economy will eventually be a balance between communism and capitalism. In a CNN report in February of this year (1992), an interview with a Soviet colonel revealed the same thing.

What I see happening in Russia today was foreseen years ago by astrologer Alice Bailey: "Out of Russia will emerge a new and magical religion," Bailey said in the 1940's. "It will be the product between humanity and hierarchy. A great spiritual religion will appear which will justify the crucifixion of that great nation."

Another prophesy was given by Edgar Cayce. Under hypnosis, Cayce said in 1932: "On Russia's religious development will come the greater hope of the world." Cayce elaborated even more in 1944: "In Russia comes the hope of the world. Freedom that each man will live for his fellow man. The principle has been born. It will take years for it to be crystallized, but out of Russia comes again the hope of the world."

When I returned home from my Soviet trip, I found out that the tribe had passed a resolution to transfer me. They waited until I was out of the country to initiate this action. Tribal officials said I was away from my job too often, but I think the reason was just pure jealousy. My fellow Sun dancers and the School Boards of Standing Rock supported me, though. They went to the tribal council and had the resolution overturned. Two or three individuals on the council were extremely bitter about having their resolution overturned, and as a result, they used their positions with the tribe, which kept trying to interfere in the day-to-day management of the BIA Education Program. Such activity is against federal law. The position that the BIA in Washington, D.C. wanted local agencies to take was to have tribal input. But the tribes misunderstood this to mean that they were now the supervisors of local BIA operations.

Because of the difficulty with the tribal council and the tribe's constant interference, I could not perform my job to full capacity, and I decided to resign. After seven years on Standing Rock, I resigned and accepted a Superintendency in South Dakota. We decided to go to the Pine Ridge

Reservation because it was my wife, Dorothy's home community, and her twin daughters were now teaching there.

INDIVIDUATION

During our lives together, Dorothy and I have had a lot of giveaways. We hosted giveaways for many different events. We had a big giveaway for Grandpa Brave Eagle's memorial. In the traditional Lakota way, a year after one passes on, it is customary to have a memorial--prayers for that person's spirit. Then the family puts on a feed and hosts a giveaway. We had naming ceremonies for the twins, where there was a giveaway; and we had adoption ceremonies for my brother, Claude Two Elk and my son, Stanley Natchez, where we had a big giveaway; and even when I graduated with my doctorate degree, we had a large giveaway. We loaded up a small U-Haul trailer with items we had gotten in Denver, brought it back to Wakpamni Lake on the Fourth of July and had a giveaway. When I finished my fourth year at the Sun Dance, we hosted a big feed and giveaway. But the largest feed and giveaway we held was when my brothers and I, with our families, held a ceremony for our folks' 50th wedding anniversary. In the traditional Lakota way, when an individual or family has an accomplishment, they realize that all abilities come from God. Responding appropriately, they would put on a feed for everyone and give to the less fortunate. The more a person gave, the better they would feel for it.

In the spring of 1989, I was invited to lecture in France on my book, *Mitakuye Oyasin* . One day, Dorothy and I were visiting the Notre Dame Cathedral in Paris. I had my hair in braids and was wearing a ribbon shirt. French people would stop and watch me walk by. It was sunny that day, with not a cloud in the sky. In fact, there was nothing in the sky except one pigeon. All of a sudden, the bird let loose a dropping. *Splat!* It landed on my head. "Why me?" I asked. "Out of a million people in Paris, why me?"

Dorothy replied, "The spirits made that piegon do that to you because of the way you were walking around acting like an "Indian chief." We had a good laugh, and I decided to tone down my prancing a little.

Dorothy and I really enjoyed our little "April in Paris" that year. We visited the Eiffel Tower, Notre Dame Cathedral, Sacred Heart Hill/Church, cabarets named Moulin Rouge and Crazy Horse, Arc de Triomphe and the Champs Élysées Boulevard shops.

In the summer of 1990 at the Sun Dance, I told the participants there the reason I planned to pull seven buffalo skulls, as I had done for Dawson at the 1981 Sun Dance. The story I told was that I had witnessed a car accident earlier that summer. We were just coming back from Rapid City, heading toward the reservation when a car went around us doing about 90 mph. I noticed it was some people from the reservation who appeared to be drinking. We got

172

about three miles down the road and found their car in the ditch. They had wrecked. It was a terrible accident! We stopped; I ran down to the car; the dust was just settling. The two people in the car were completely mangled. The boy had part of his face gone, his chest was crushed and his legs were all mangled. The girl's head from her forehead back had been gashed open and it looked like she had been scalped. It was terrible! A man with a car phone arrived and called the police. As we waited for the police and ambulance, I remember how helpless I felt about this situation. I picked four sprigs of sage and said a prayer for the victims. All of a sudden, a force came around the boy, whirling above him for about a minute, then lifting up and disappearing. I believe it was the spirits who had come to receive the boy's spirit into the spirit world. Shortly after this, the ambulance arrived and took the two to the hospital.

As a result of witnessing this accident, I felt that drinking is just a symptom of something deeper that is happening to our Lakota people. I feel that it's not really the people's fault what is happening to them. I therefore pulled the skulls to learn why alcohol is affecting 100% of the people on the reservation. During that year, I gained information about the leading causes of alcoholism on the reservation. We have high unemployment. Congress provides us with welfare payments. Then there is welfare abuse, many people using their welfare money for drinking. As stated earlier, I found out that here in the United States one percent of the people own over half the money. They control the economy, the labor, the jobs; they even control Congress and the President. There is no work on the reservations, and in our capitalist society, the bottom line is the profit motive, making a dollar. People don't want to bring industry or work to the reservation because they don't see any profit in it. Thus, we end up with no jobs and as a result, we have to move to wherever there's work. Well, this welfare mentality is killing us. Sure, we need the money, but what Congress should do is to have the people work for their money rather than just give it to them. There are many jobs we could do on the reservation. A lot of places that we could help. In the schools alone, we need bus monitors, we need hall monitors, cooks' helpers, classroom aides. We need all kinds of help. Menial jobs could be established so we could do work for the welfare money.

I found out that this capitalist system we live in has been unfair. This is what is being exposed now. In the past several years, we've had Ivan Boesky, Mike Milken, Charles Keating--all these people who have been uncovered for misusing the capitalist system. The rich get richer, the poor stay poor. If someone wants to start a business and needs a loan to do it, that person needs to know somebody or have collateral to get a loan. That's why, in the past, the influential would get loans and the poor would stay poor.

The average person who works is required to pay taxes. They're the ones who have to foot the bill for welfare. And the rich have influenced Congress to where they don't have to pay their share of taxes. It's an unfair system, but we live in a democracy and it's only the people themselves who can change it. All we need to do is put these issues on a ballot and vote on them. That's what needs to happen.

In the fall of 1990, I attended an NIEA conference in San Diego. I was taking garlic tablets so I wouldn't catch the flu. Well, I started to get a gout attack one evening. When I took my gout medication, Endocin, it mixed with the garlic tablets (this is what I believe) and caused a reaction. It was like I had a drug overdose. I was on the verge of flipping out. I felt evil just waiting for me to give in, but I wouldn't. I called a friend of mine, John Around Him. It was about 1:00 in the morning, and I said, "I've got to walk, John, I've got to walk." It was like everything was closing in on me. He came over and we started to walk. We got as far as the lobby. I was afraid of going outside, so he walked me around in a circle for almost three hours until I wore the drugs off. I was holding my pipe as John walked with me. Finally, he got tired and sat down, but I just kept walking and kept praying.

This incident happened to me accidently; but I wondered if people who overdose on heroin or cocaine have similar experiences. I thought to myself, "If this is true, then I can relate to people who overdose on drugs." It is so easy to give up and go to the other side, but I didn't want to give up. I felt I had not completed my evolutionary journey yet. That's the reason I just kept praying and holding onto my pipe, hoping to stay alive. If I left this earthly plane without completing my evolutionary journey, I would only be sent back to try again. This I don't want. I want to finish this time.

The winter of 1990, people commemorated the 100th-year anniversary of the Wounded Knee Massacre by holding a memorial 200-mile ride on horseback. The ride followed the same path that Chief Big Foot had taken 100 years previous. One of the organizers for the ride was Birgil Kills Straight, who was, in the Lakota way, my brother-in-law. So I volunteered to help.

I was a rider in charge of the wagon, the tent crew, the pow-wow, and the meals that we served at the school. Consequently, my wife and I were very busy running around during the ride. Each morning, the riders would gather in a circle on horseback. Arvol Looking Horse, Keeper of the Pipe, would pray for the deceased of 1890; then one of the leaders would explain what additional cause we would be riding for. One day, we rode for women's rights, another day for orphaned children, other days for other such causes.

I had a very unusual experience during the ride. I had on long johns, a pair of pants, and winter coveralls over these. I wore a T-shirt, a turtleneck pullover, a winter jacket and a riding duster. I didn't get cold except for my feet and my face. I had a ski mask on, but the wind blew right through it. I had boots on, even though I knew they would be cold. The previous year, I had worn snow boots; my feet didn't get cold, but my ankles were rubbed raw from the stirrups. By wearing boots this year, my ankles didn't hurt, but my feet got cold. It was about 35° below zero on the third day of the ride. I was wearing my ski mask and like Dr. Jung, the psychologist, says, "When you have a mask on, it becomes your persona." When I wore the ski mask, nobody knew who I was. During that day, it seemed as though I had become possessed. A force had taken over my body. It was like I wasn't tired, I wasn't cold. I felt really strange. Then I recognized what it must be like to be a masked dancer in a ceremony. I had lost my identity, another force had taken over my body, and I became an excellent horseman. My horse was named Hondo. I felt very good about how he performed that day. During the ride, I didn't want to tell anybody this was happening to me because I thought if I did, the force would leave. I waited until after the ride to share the story.

I went on the Wounded Knee Memorial Ride mainly because of my belief in traditional D/Lakota philosophy and thought. Edgar Cayce, the psychic healer, prophesied that there are five things a person must do in order to finish his or her evolutionary journey on earth. As I studied these five components, I came to know that they are identical to concepts in traditional Native American philosophy and thought. I want to share these connections between Cayce's and the D/Lakota designations. They are also my reasons for participating in the ride.

The first reason is brotherly love. Cayce said one must exhibit brotherly love for all things, not only other people but also the four-leggeds, the winged ones, the creatures in the water, even the rocks. If a person can truly love a rock like a brother, that's one of the things we need to do in order to finish our evolutionary journey here on the planet. In the Lakota way, we don't have a book that tells us these things, but we have ceremonies where we do these things. The most sacred item in D/Lakota spirituality is a rock pipe. We cherish that rock pipe, we honor it, we have respect for it. In the Lakota way, we have sacred rock mountains that are held in respect. They, in turn, represent Mother Earth, which is also made of rock. We learn to love this Earth. We learn to love these mountains. We learn to love the rock like we love a brother. The rock, the mountains, Mother Earth herself are simply three different aspects of the same entity.

The second reason is peace. It is necessary to always strive for peace, no matter what situation one is in. The sacred rock pipe is always used in peace, to strive for peace. We never used it to start war.

The third reason is patience. We have sacred ceremonies where we learn to develop and achieve patience. There are two types of patience, passive patience and active patience. Passive patience is the one I am most familiar with. This is where one learns to sit back and wait. Active patience is where a person learns to go with the flow, learns to follow intuitions and instincts, learns to go with one's feelings. One ceremony for developing both types of patience is the Vision Quest where one goes up on a mountaintop for four days and four nights. No food and no water--a person just waits there, with one's pipe and one's prayers. The quester waits for a vision or dream. The dream or vision will guide that person in what he or she is to be doing in this life.

The fourth reason is the ability to endure difficult situations. A philosophy in D/Lakota thought is that everything goes in cycles. If one is good to people, that will come back. If one is wicked to people, that's also going to come back. I remember a Lakota story about two boys who were playing and got into a fight. One boy killed the other. The parents of the dead boy really felt bad about their loss and wanted to know what to do. They went to the elders, who told them they should now adopt the murderer as their son and raise him in place of their son. That's how they could get through this situation.

Similarly, in the film "Gandhi," a Hindu man approached Gandhi and reported that the Moslems had killed his son. He, in turn, had killed a Moslem youth. Gandhi told the man if he wanted to rid himself of this negative karma, he needed to find an orphaned Moslem boy the same age his son was and raise him as his own. However, he had to raise this boy as a Moslem, even though he was a Hindu.

Indian people have ceremonies that originate from a very old philosophy where they learn to endure difficult situations; for instance, the sweat lodge, vision quest, Sun Dance. An example from everyday life: maybe a person can't get along with a boss or a co-worker, or maybe a person is struggling with one's spouse. Whatever the situation is, we need to learn to endure these circumstances and work our way through them. If we don't, that problem will appear the next time we come into Earth's plane. If one thinks there is an escape from these difficulties, one is just fooling oneself.

The fifth reason is balance and harmony. We call that walking the Red Road in D/Lakota philosophy, walking in balance. Everything in our way of thinking is in pairs of opposites--good and bad, light and dark, night and day, male and female. Only *Tuŋkašila/Wakaŋ Taŋka* (Grandfather/Great Spirit) is both. We need to walk in balance. If we go to one extreme or another, then we're going to throw ourselves out of balance. A good example is the movie "Elmer Gantry." The main character preached holier-than-thou Biblical teachings during the day. He became so holier-than-thou that he threw himself out of balance and, in the evening, became a whiskey-drinking, girl-chasing individual. That's what happens when a person goes to extremes.

Traditional Lakota ceremonies provide a balanced way of life. The elders tell us, for example, that someone goes in the sweat lodge to suffer so that they'll have good answers to their prayers. It's very hot in there and the person is really suffering. That's the negative part, but the positive part is that then one will receive good answers to one's prayers.

Another example is that of AIDS, which we generally think of as a very bad disease. Yet, seeing the balance, we could say that AIDS allows the soul to experience suffering, thus enabling that soul to gain on its path toward completion of its evolutionary journey. Another positive aspect is that the disease is causing people to become more spiritual, since there is no medical cure.

I went on the ride to pray for the deceased, to pray for those who were murdered 100 years ago, to help their spirits. By praying for their spirits, we can help them finish their evolutionary journey. By my riding and praying for them, I'm helping them, but at the same time, I'm helping myself complete my evolutionary journey on earth. That's what D/Lakota philosophy and thought is all about.

Big Foot Ride Prophecy

In the spring, I had an operation to remove a growth from my right elbow that had been caused by my gout. As a result of the operation, I sustained nerve damage to my right arm; consequently, I have a disability in that arm. I have gout-related arthritis that has now spread to my knees, feet and hands. I can no longer sit cross-legged for any length of time. I am even beginning to find it difficult to sit for very long in the sweat lodge. After the second round, I need to straighten my legs. No matter what I try to rid myself of this arthritis, nothing really helps. A wounded healer?

I was attending a pow-wow in Rapid City, South Dakota in 1991. I had a booth where I was selling my books and Lakota language tapes. A man came to the booth, picked up the book, and was looking through it. He stopped at the chapter about the UFO connection, read a few pages, and then put the book down, looking at me, and said, "The people from the Pleiades are really magnificent people." Then he added, "Did you know that you have spirit guides?"

"Yes," I answered.

He declared, "You have three of them."

I said, "Yes, I know that. I put it in the book." As I looked at him, I noticed that just before he'd say something, the irises of his eyes turned upward and to the left. I knew right then that when he performed that action, he was getting in tune with the spirit world so they would tell him certain things.

He again looked up in the corner of his eyes, looked back at me and said, "The spirit guides are trying to get in contact with you. You need to spend more time being in touch with them."

I replied, "I know that; I've been pushing myself too much lately, and I'd like to spend more time as you suggest." I thanked him. He and his wife were standing there, and it was like there was a totally different aura feeling coming from them than what I've felt from most people. After he left, I mentioned the incident to Dorothy, and I said, "I wonder if those two were UFO people themselves." But then I answered my own conjecture: "Well, maybe not. I think he was simply a psychic because I could tell by his eyes when he was getting in touch with the spirit world." After telling my wife what he had said, we just let the matter be.

Dorothy was extremely happy to return to her home community on the Pine Ridge Reservation, but once we got back, she found out it was completely different from the way she had visualized it from her youth.

At the school where I was employed on Pine Ridge, I recognized that the school board had allowed staff and community members to circumvent administration and go straight to them with any problems. The administrator at the school was only a figurehead. The school board wanted to be the administrators and they interfered with administrative duties. I had an incident with a school employee. When the school board heard of it, they immediately suspended me without a hearing. I found out later that the employee was related to a person on the school board who pushed to have me suspended.

Friends in the community circulated a petition on my behalf. They gathered over 300 signatures, then gave the petition to the school board. I hired a lawyer and we went to a school board hearing. Based on the testimony of a previous superintendent of the school as to the conduct of the employee I had had the problem with, the embarrassed school board was required to reinstate me and give me my back pay. Once I received my back pay, I immediately resigned.

When this trouble with the school board started, I went to Elmer Running, a Medicine Man from Rosebud, and had a ceremony. In the ceremony the spirits told him that everything was going to be all right for me. The school board was going to give me my job back and he told me not to worry. Also in the ceremony, the spirits told him there was a person at the school who had had a ceremony to send bad medicine to me, creating this whole mess. I still wonder, to this day, who could have hated me so much that they would misuse a sacred ceremony to have bad medicine sent against me.

I decided to leave educational administration because of the school board's lack of knowledge in their role as policy makers versus their assumed role as administrators. I started my own consultant firm, where I promote my book, give lectures, presentations, and book signings.

When I resigned my job on the Pine Ridge Reservation, my wife was still working for the BIA but was forced into resigning her position because of an obsolete law that was established back when the Indian agents and reservation superintendents were corrupt. At that time, the agents were usually political appointees who tried to take advantage of local Indian populations, taking their money. To counteract the practice, a law was established that BIA employees and their families were forbidden to carry on any trade or dealings with the Indians. It's called "Trading with the Indians Clause." Well, the law is still on the books. When I began my own consultant firm and publishing company, Dorothy contacted the BIA Aberdeen Area Office Personnel Department, who informed her that they thought the old law applied to her. She argued that it was her husband, not she, who had set up the business. The authority in Aberdeen said, "Well, you're still family, so it applies to you." We wrote to the solicitor to get an opinion. He said that the law still applied. It just seemed totally unfair to us that Dorothy had to resign her job with the BIA because of an outdated law. We weren't trading with the Indians, we weren't out trying to rip off anyone, yet the law still applied to us.

Our company name is BEAR, an acronym for Brave Eagle Allen Ross. (Brave Eagle is my wife's family name.) Then, come to find out, the name is also very close to Dawson No Horse's Indian name--Holy Bear.

In the fall of 1991, we were doing a show in San Jose, CA. One evening, Dorothy awoke with chest pains and numbness in her arms. We went to the emergency room at the hospital. The staff put her on an EKG machine, and it recorded that she was having a heart attack. I said, "I don't believe it." We decided to leave and get a second opinion. But the doctor scared Dorothy into staying for twenty-four-hour observation. A second EKG showed nothing, and the medical conclusion was that it must be stomach gas. The following week, we went to our doctor in Denver, who deduced that the problem was a hiatal hernia. Dorothy started treatment for it, but the numbness in her hand remained. Our doctor referred us to a neurologist.

That doctor said it was a brain tumor, scaring Dorothy half to death. A brain scan proved it was not. Then the neurologist speculated, "Well, I think you have Parkinson's disease."

I told Dorothy, "Let's go home and have a ceremony. This doctor is just guessing. Meanwhile, she is charging us hundreds of dollars for her guesswork."

I thought, "Why is this neurologist charging so much money? If she has a gift from God to do healing, why aren't her services free, like what the Lakota Medicine People practice?"

We had a sweat lodge ceremony, and I used the technique we had used for Joe Weiler. This time, I asked Rolland Williston to help me. The spirits informed him that there was no problem in the brain area. They did tell him, though, that Dorothy was having difficulties where the esophagus meets the stomach. The spirits then directed him in repairing the area. Afterwards, Rolland asked me who the woman was he had worked on. I told him it was Dorothy. He said he had seen her in the sweat. The next day, she said she was feeling better. When we returned to Denver, she went to a nutritional therapist, who put her on a nutritional yeast-free diet so the problem would not recur.

However, the numbness in Dorothy's hand remained. Since we were constantly traveling from presentation to presentation, we could not have a sweat lodge ceremony. Instead, we decided to seek the advice of a psychic because we believe that such a person receives their information from the spirit world as well. (A key to visiting a psychic is to not tell that person where one is hurt or has pain. By the client giving no clues, the psychic must use his or her powers to identify the problem.) The psychic told Dorothy to see a chiropractor because she felt there was a disturbance in the neck area. The chiropractor x-rayed Dorothy's neck and found an improper alignment. He said it was from an old injury. We wondered if it had been caused by the accident when the drunken tribal employee had rear-ended our van a few years back. Anyway, after receiving proper adjustments for her neck, Dorothy's strength in her hand and arm is now returning.

The 1991 NIEA Conference was held in Omaha. The official position of the National Indian Education Association was, as presented in a paper, to endorse wholistic education. Well, when I heard that, I felt great because I had introduced wholistic education to NIEA back in 1979 and had really promoted the approach through workshops over the years. Now it has become official doctrine. Because of my achievement, one of the leaders at the conference came up to me and said, "Dr. Ross, I've been following you now for the last ten years and I really admire what you're doing. I just wanted to say thank you for the work you're doing in helping us in the field of education." He added, "I think you need to hear that from us." I was very pleased and thanked him for his comments.

My tribe, the Flandreau Santee Sioux, built a gambling casino and are currently making approximately $750,000 a month on the proceeds. The money to build the casino came from land claims awarded to the tribe. The tribe voted to pay each member residing on the reservation $1,000 per month. The problem is that only members living on the reservation could vote on the issue. The tribe has an enrollment around 500, but only about 100 actually live on the reservation. Because of this unfair method of paying the dividends to only a few members of the tribe, I decided to initiate a lawsuit against the tribe. I'm not concerned about the money; it is the principle of the matter that bothers me. It appears that greed was the motive for the tribe's actions.

I blame the economic system in this country. I call it "unfair practices of capitalism" where the bottom line is the profit motive. Here in America, it is called "the American Dream." I feel the American Dream is just a sales gimmick to entice people to buy. We live in a credit card society. Almost anything can be purchased on credit (but the catch is the amount of interest one pays to do so). This method of enticement is a deterrent to poor people. They are surrounded by advertisements to buy. Naturally, they want material goods also. The poorer they are, the more they want. It is reverse psychology working against the poor. The poor are poor, to begin with, because of the unfair method of gaining wealth in this country. (One needs money to borrow money, as stated previously. The system keeps the poor at an economic disadvantage, then turns around and condemns them for being poor.) If Jesus were alive today, He would be very upset because it is said that this is precisely the reason He went into the temple and turned over the money tables. (The money lenders were making money on interest by enticing the public to borrow.)

A couple of months ago, I was in Fort Lauderdale, Florida for a show. The taxicab driver who drove me to the display area asked me what prophecies the Indian people have about these last days. I told him there would be changes in the economy, the government, and in spirituality. He asked, "Do you think there will be a revolution in this country?"

I answered, "The revolution is already occurring. It is happening at the voting booths." This was two months before the discovery of the Congressional bank scandal! Is the United States finally experiencing individuation by admitting her weaknesses? At least, this is a beginning for achieving wholeness.

EPILOGUE

When Dakota Territory was divided into North and South Dakota, the western half of South Dakota was set aside as a reservation for the Teton Sioux. Through a series of treaties, this reservation was greatly reduced in size. Finally, in the Treaty of 1876, the sacred Black Hills of the Sioux were taken away illegally. Presently, there's a bill in Congress to return the Black Hills to the Sioux. The Senate Select Committee on Indian Affairs, which is made up of senators from states with large American Indian populations, has decided that they will not act on the bill as long as the senator from South Dakota is opposed to the bill. Unfortunately, the senator is strongly influenced by the tourist industry in South Dakota. The tourist industry does not want the Black Hills returned to the Sioux, primarily because that is where their largest attractions lie.

Another reason for the state not wanting the tribal councils to gain control of the Black Hills is that according to the 1990 census, 63% of American Indians now live off the reservation, leaving only 37% to reside on the reservations. The 1990 census also indicated that those who left the reservation were those with education and training. It appears, then, that there has been a brain drain from the reservations. (Currently, some tribal councils are in a state of chaos and are filled with corruption.)

The solution, according to my vision of the butterfly (*Mitakuye Oyasin*, pp. 192-193), was that we should return to the original teachings if we are to survive. Tribal councils and other governing bodies on the reservations should establish standards and codes of conduct with a means of retribution for those who do not follow them.

The tribes need to address the off-reservation issue. Every member of the tribes should be allowed to vote, whether they live on or off reservations. Agreements should be made among Sioux reservations to allow voting rights for non-member Sioux who live on the reservations. After all, the government created the reservations that have divided our tribe.

Tribes also need to become self-sufficient. There is a need for tribal councils to start imposing taxes on the members of the tribes. Traditionally, the Lakota people had a taxing system, as well as standard codes of conduct.

The traditional system of taxation was conducted by the following method: the Soldier Society that was selected to head the tribe for that year would come out in the village center and sing society songs. Then they would go around the camp circle and sing doorway songs. If they placed a staff in front of a particular tipi and sang doorway songs, that meant that the tipi owner had to donate to the society. The Soldier Society went around the camp collecting the donations and brought them back out into the center of the camp circle. Then they called out the individuals who had made the donations and sang honor songs for them. Next, they took the donations and gave them to the old, the sick, the poor, the crippled. It was a system of taxation, though we didn't call it that. We called it the give-away system, a means for equally distributing the tribal wealth. It was the system we used and it worked. Jesus spoke of this method of sharing when a merchant asked Him, "What can I do to be your servant?" Jesus responded that the man should give away everything he had in order to follow Him.

Traditional Lakota codes of conduct were used in selecting tribal leaders. An example: traditionally, tribal council membership was made up of Civil Societies, Soldier Societies, and Dream Societies. When a man from a Civil Society was to be considered for membership on the tribal council, he had to prove his spirituality by carrying hot rocks in his bare hands into the council tipi. If he could do this without becoming burned, then they knew he was in connection with the Great Spirit, and therefore was entitled to hold office.

Another practice held for membership was that if a man from the Dream Society could put his hand in boiling water without getting burned, the people knew this man was in connection with the spirit energy and therefore he was entitled to hold office.

The question arises: how many tribal council members could pass these tests nowadays?

Three suggestions for the return for the Black Hills:
1) Return the land to the tribes with the understanding that it would be subject to taxation.

2) Return the Black Hills to a Sioux Indian business committee, made up of educated, competent individuals of Sioux descent (one-half Indian or more), who possess traditional D/Lakota values, who speak Dakota or Lakota, and who practice D/Lakota religion. These individuals would head up the committee that would manage the sacred Black Hills for the D/Lakota people.

3) Use a method that is being used in Australia. The Australian government has returned large tracts of land to the Aborigines with the understanding that the Aborigines lease it back to them immediately. The land now belongs to the Aborigines and they are now getting lease money for it.

Even though I have made these suggestions, I know that none of them will be agreed upon by the tribes. This is due, I think, primarily to the influence of tribal attorneys, many of whom are non-Indian and want to keep the tribes and the Indian state of affairs in confusion. I think that this is largely so that they can keep drawing a salary from the tribes.

The problems in D/Lakota country today are not unique to D/Lakota people. Such challenges are worldwide, caused by greed and selfishness on the part of individuals. As Dr. Carl Jung stated, "Modern man is ego-oriented." We are living for ourselves. I feel we need to live for our fellow humans if we are to survive as a people on this planet.

One night after I had done the first draft of this book, I had a dream and a voice called me. I realized it was the same voice that had called in the Biblical story of Samuel. This was also the same situation with Dorothy when the voice called her name from the basement. When I heard the voice call my name, I knew what it was, and I said, like Eli had advised Samuel, "Speak, Master, for I am your servant." Then I went back to sleep. Maybe it is the voices from the spirit world who have helped me write this second book.

With all the problems that I had with tribal councils and school boards, I have no feelings of revenge. From studying the psychology of people, I know the situation they're in and how they react to their circumstances. The archetype of power is a term from psychology. When a person who has never had any position of authority is suddenly given one, the power archetype penetrates consciousness and then controls that person. One of the best examples I can recall on TV was on the "Andy Griffith Show." He gave his deputy, Barney Fife, authority, only to have it abused. Andy then gave Barney just one bullet and told the deputy to carry it in his pocket so he wouldn't misuse the power. Similarly, a lot of people who never had training and never had education in psychology don't realize that the archetype of power overtakes them and they do things without realizing what they're doing. I know and understand why people do things to harm me, and so, I just let the matter be.

I remember what the Bible said when the soldiers and people were spitting on Christ and crucified him. He said, "Father, forgive them, for they know not what they do."

This is the same sort of situation for me. I have no qualms about what others did to me, even though throughout my lifetime, I've been discriminated against by whites, blacks, other Indian tribes, and now by my own tribe.

The old Indian way, as I mentioned before, is that it is more honorable to touch one's enemy than it is to kill him. The traditional people never sought revenge. In the Bible, the Lord says, "Vengeance is mine." This tells me that people who seek revenge on others will get their due in their own time for whatever they've done. That's why it's important to just let things be. That's the way they're supposed to be. Furthermore, a person is in his or her own situation through personal choice. Each knew before his or her spirit ever came into Earth's plane what he or she was getting into. There is no reason, therefore, to blame anybody else. All we can do to help others is to serve as an example for them.

A lot of people died in the Minnesota eight-week war of 1862. Over 500 settlers and soldiers and an unknown number of Santee Sioux died. That situation happened because it was supposed to happen. People come into Earth's plane to have a chance to meet their karma, to deal with deeds done in previous lives which come back on them in this life. The best way to remedy the situation or to meet one's karma is to deal directly with it. Each life we come into Earth's plane, we come here for a different reason, to experience certain things. After these experiences, through a number of lifetimes, we are able to finish our evolutionary journeys here on the planet, as discussed earlier.

With that thought in mind, I would like to offer a prayer for all the people who died in the conflict in Minnesota in 1862-63. I'd like to pray for all people to gain a better understanding of their purpose on earth, and I ask *Tuŋkašila* to help the spirits of the deceased so they can complete their evolutionary journey. I'd like to offer a prayer to help all people to know that they, too, can finish their evolutionary journeys. These things I ask at this time. *Mitakuye Oyasin.*

ORDER FORM

Name _____

Address _____

City _____ State _____ Zip _____

Qty	Title	Price/Book	Total
	EHANAMANI		
	MITAKUYE OYASIN		
SUBTOTAL			
	Postage (see below)		
	Handling ($1.50 per order)		
TOTAL			

<u>Prices for both books</u>   <u>Postage (book rate)</u>

 1 copy $12.00 each   1-3 copies $ 1.50 per book

 2-10 copies   11.00 each   4 or more copies   .50 per book

or more copies 10.00 each

Mail: For orders outside the U.S., add $5.00 per book. For other ernational orders, add $8.00 per book.

ke checks, money orders and
chase orders payable to: For wholesale orders, contact:

Wichóni Wasté   Ingram Book Co.   (800) 937-8000
BOX 480005   P.O. Box 3006
DENVER, CO 80248   LaVergne, TN 37086-1986

--NO CREDIT CARD ORDERS--

ABOUT THE AUTHOR

Dr. A.C. Ross was named *Ehanamani* (Walks Among) in a Dakota ceremony. Ehanamani is a patrilineal family name. Great-Grandfather Artemus Ehanamani was put in prison at Fort Snelling, Minnesota after the eight-week war of 1862. Upon release, he went to Santee, Nebraska and joined his sister, my Great-Grandmother Maggie Ehanamani. Maggie married John Frasier and Artemus married John's sister. Because of the anti-Indian pressure at that time, Artemus and Maggie changed their names to Frasier.

The present Ehanamani (Dr. Ross) has worked for 25 years in the field of education as a teacher, principal, superintendent, college professor, and college department chairman. He has lectured on cultural understanding in 44 states in the U.S., 6 Canadian provinces, and 5 European countries. His book, *Mitakuye Oyasin/We Are All Related*, is currently a best-seller.